T0318258

Impact in International Affairs

This book examines how and to what extent academic research in politics and international studies has had 'impact' — in doing so, it also considers what might characterise 'world-leading' research impact.

International Relations was always meant to have impact — it was intended to make a difference in the world, when the subject was formally founded to understand and prevent war in 1919. This volume addresses the concept of 'impact' and offers a typology of the term — instrumental, conceptual, capacity building and procedural. The authors examine 111 impact case studies in the UK Research Excellence Framework (2014) that were classified as having achieved the highest level of evaluation, and they identify eight characteristics that mark 'world-leading' impact. The book concludes that process and public and media engagement are previously underestimated aspects of impact in official approaches. It further demonstrates that achieving the top levels of impact in international relations is possible, but that factors such as the nature of the subject, the approach of researchers and mean-spiritedness in the peer review process inhibited this.

This book will be of much interest to students of politics and international studies, as well as educational research and policy makers, and anyone interested in, or working on, research impact.

James Gow is Professor of International Peace and Security at King's College London, UK.

Henry Redwood is Lecturer in International Relations at King's College London, UK.

Impact in International Affairs

The Quest for World-Leading Research

James Gow and Henry Redwood

Routledge
Taylor & Francis Group

LONDON AND NEW YORK

First published 2021
by Routledge
2 Park Square, Milton Park, Abingdon, Oxon OX14 4RN

and by Routledge
52 Vanderbilt Avenue, New York, NY 10017

Routledge is an imprint of the Taylor & Francis Group, an informa business

British Library Cataloguing-in-Publication Data
A catalogue record for this book is available from the British Library

Library of Congress Cataloging-in-Publication Data

Names: Gow, James, author. | Redwood, Henry, 1988- author.

Title: Impact in international affairs: the quest for world-leading research/James Gow and Henry Redwood.

Description: Abingdon, Oxon; New York, NY: Routledge, 2021. | Includes bibliographical references and index.

Identifiers: LCCN 2020013904 (print) | LCCN 2020013905 (ebook) | ISBN 9780367902032 (hardback) | ISBN 9781003023081 (ebook)

Subjects: LCSH: International relations–Research–Case studies.

Classification: LCC JZ1234 .G68 2021 (print) | LCC JZ1234 (ebook) | DDC 327.072–dc23

LC record available at https://lccn.loc.gov/2020013904
LC ebook record available at https://lccn.loc.gov/2020013905

ISBN: 978-0-367-90203-2 (hbk)
ISBN: 978-0-367-53942-9 (pbk)
ISBN: 978-1-003-02308-1 (ebk)

Typeset in Times New Roman
by MPS Limited, Dehradun

Contents

Tables

Preface

We wish to acknowledge the excellent support, help and research assistance of Ernst Dijxhoorn, while at King's College London, when early thinking about 'impact' was developing; he moved on to pursue other agendas at Leiden University. We also wish to thank two Steven Hills for their interest, encouragement and help — one from Research England, who accidentally set this project going, and the other formerly of the UK Diplomatic Service and now Credit Suisse. In addition, we are grateful to the School of Security Studies at King's College London and its Director, Professor Wyn Bowen, in particular, for funding the Research Associate post (from funds allocated by the Faculty of Social Science and Public Policy) that gave Henry the opportunity to become engaged, initially, as Research Associate on impact, and also Professor Mike Goodman, who supported this. We are also grateful to the many colleagues with whom we have worked on research projects that have made differences in the world and who have supported us, most notably Rachel Kerr, Tiffany Fairey and Milena Michalski at King's, and Elma Hašimbegović, Elma Hodžić and Velma Šarić in Bosnia, on two remarkable AHRC-PaCCS-GCRF-funded projects, both of which explored impact in practice: 'Art and Reconciliation: Conflict Culture and Community' (AH/P005365/1), on which we both worked; and 'Art and Reconciliation', AHRC-GCRF 'Art and Reconciliation — Open Calls and the Living Museum: Innovation, Research and the History Museum of Bosnia and Hercegovina' (AH/S005641/1), on which only the more senior of us worked. We are also pleased to acknowledge the general benefit to this project of various other projects that benefited from AHRC and ESRC funding that we received.

1 Introduction

International Relations was always meant to have impact.[1] That is, research under that umbrella was intended to make a difference in the world.[2] First established formally at the University of Wales, Aberystwyth, in 1919, through the creation of an academic chair with that title, by a liberal political figure, David Davies, in the wake of the First World War, its mission was to understand the causes of war and to use that understanding to outlaw war.[3] Of course, that was a mission impossible.[4] But, it made clear the intended purpose, as with medicine, not simply to know and understand, but to improve the world, even if, as some scholars observed, there could be hidden or inadvertent, or problematic, consequences, whether in terms of race, colonialism, or wider security

---

1 'Impact' is a key term in the present study. Throughout, we use it, fairly simply, to mean research 'making a difference' in the world. Although 'impact' is used, generally, it should be understood that this always means 'research impact' in the relevant contexts. We have tried to eschew any other use of 'impact' to avoid confusion. As a term, a subject and an agenda, it is discussed below, in this Introduction and, more fully, in Chapter 2.

2 We wish to acknowledge the support and help and of all those mentioned in the Preface, as well as research funding from the School of Security Studies and SSPP, King's College London; AHRC-PaCCS-GCRF 'Art and Reconciliation: Conflict Culture and Community' (AH/P005365/1); and 'Art and Reconciliation', AHRC-GCRF 'Art and Reconciliation — Open Calls and the Living Museum: Innovation, Research and the History Museum of Bosnia and Hercegovina' (AH/S005641/1).

3 We offer a summary of International Relations, as a field, and an essential history of the creation of the Chair at Aberystwyth, below.

4 See Michael Howard, *War and the Liberal Conscience*, London: Clarendon, 1979 and Revised Ed. London: Hurst and Co., 2008, for an unmatchable account of the enduring and almost ever-present phenomenon of war, and seemingly inevitable failures of attempts to eradicate it — each attempt preceding armed conflict worse than anything that had gone before.

practices.[5] Writing a century later, we might take on the responsibility to evaluate in which ways and to what extent that mission had any success — and, perhaps, as we write, someone, somewhere has no doubt taken on that grand challenge. Certainly, many examinations of a hundred years of International Relations must have been drafted, as we were writing this volume.[6] But, maybe none of them would consider that original sense of making a difference in the world,[7] even if the core ambition to eliminate war might have been too unrealistic.

Moreover, as well as that historic desire to improve the world, even more, there was the increasing expectation outside research institutions — from funders, governments and publics — that some research should be having impact in the world. In the UK, impact (examined as a concept in Chapter 2) emerged slowly in the 2000s, began to be seriously discussed around 2010, and was firmly at the centre of the agenda by 2014. Its emergence as part of a formal, bureaucratic evaluation exercise in the UK was an innovation that others would start to follow. The research impact agenda quickly came to have wide international purchase. Funding bodies in other European countries, such as Finland, Sweden,[8] the Netherlands[9] and

---

5 See Duncan Bell, 'Writing the World', *International Affairs* Vol. 85 No. 1 2009, pp. 3–22; and Robbie Shillam *et al.,* eds., *Race and Racism in International Relations,* London: Routledge, 2015.

6 The major journal *International Relations,* for example, devoted a special issue to the centenary, Vol. 33, Issue 2, 2019. Among other events, a conference in Italy including major figures in the field marked the centenary. 'International Relations at 100: The Liberal World Order and Beyond', ASERI, Università Cattolica del Sacro Cuore, 15 November 2019.

7 The tendency in politics and international relations has been to focus on theory and the field of enquiry, or discipline, itself. The nature of the field is discussed briefly below, but, for now, it might be sufficient to note the extent to which discourse concerns competition between different lenses, notably the dominant ones of 'realism' and 'liberalism' (although each of these had variants and alternative names, of course), and, perhaps, later notions, such as 'constructivism' and 'critical theory.' Any introduction to studying the topic will present these positions and frame study in relation to them — just one of them, as a preferred approach, or, more openly, all of them, as a selection. See below.

8 Gemma Derrick, *The Evaluator's Eye: Impact Assessment and Academic Peer Review,* Cham: Palgrave Macmillan, 2018, p. 30.

9 The Netherlands' Standard Evaluation Protocol for universities, in 2015, considered 'relevance to society' of research and 'the quality, scale and relevance of contributions targeting specific economic, social or cultural target [*sic* — the authors] groups, of advisory reports for policy, of contributions to public debates, and so on.' Quoted by Derrick, *The Evaluator's Eye,* p. 30.

Slovenia,[10] all came to value research impact, whether as potential set out in funding proposals, or as evidence of quality in research assessed. The notion was also introduced by the European Research Council, which sought 'customer and societal benefits.'[11] Beyond Europe, Excellence in Research for Australia innovated beyond its traditional focus on research *qua* research, evaluated by peer review, to seek to 'create and embed a culture of and expectation for research impact within Australian universities and in wider society.'[12] New Zealand also entered the 'impact' arena,[13] while the US National Science Foundation had a long history of considering 'broader impacts' as a factor in its funding.[14]

It was hardly surprising that funders — often backed by governments, but even those not so — would want to see their investments have social, economic, cultural or some other benefit, given increasing trends of accountability and concomitant bureaucratisation.[15] In that sense, without having a formal 'impact' agenda, not only the US government, which had an obvious interest in practical research, but also the major US foundations, all sought to fund research that would make a difference in the world. For example, the John T. and Catherine D. MacArthur Foundation and its International Peace and Security programme,[16] was committed to funding research that might affect major issues, such as nuclear deterrence, in the Cold War, whether through its research and writing fellowships, its support for doctoral and post-doctoral work through the US SSPP (Social Science and Public Policy) Program, or via its core, long-term funding to six or seven institutions. Similarly, the Ford Foundation and the Carnegie Endowment would seek to support what it viewed as positive change in the world — and would not renew funding where there was little evidence of a difference being made.[17] The same was true of funders,

---

10 ARRS — The Slovenian Research Agency, for example, asks those making proposals to describe the 'potential impact achieved by the development, dissemination and use of the expected research results', and asks reviewers to judge that description in its evaluation process (www.arrs.si accessed at 29 July 2019).

11 Quoted in Derrick, *The Evaluator's Eye*, p. 31.

12 Quoted in Derrick, *The Evaluator's Eye*, p. 30.

13 Derrick, *The Evaluator's Eye*, p. 70.

14 Quoted in Derrick, *The Evaluator's Eye*, p. 70.

15 John O'Regan and John Gray, 'The Bureaucratic Distortion of Academic Work', *Language and Intercultural Communication* Vol. 18 No. 5 2018, pp. 533–48.

16 See www.macfound.org/tags/peace-security/ accessed at 29 July 2019.

17 The Ford Foundation www.fordfoundation.org and Carnegie Endowment https://carnegieendowment.org/programs accessed at 29 July 2019.

such as the US Institute of Peace,[18] or the US Congress-backed Woodrow Wilson International Center for Scholars,[19] with its particular focus on public policy. With the growth of the impact fashion, even smaller funders, such as the Harry Frank Guggenheim Foundation,[20] began to lose their traditional commitment to pure research on violence (not that it ever opposed research that made a difference).

Yet, despite the original purpose of the field, the history of funding committed to making a difference though research, and the growing external pressure in the 21st century, there was no focus on that issue, as such, among academics in the field. Our purpose is to provide that focus, for the first time. In the following pages, we seek to examine in which ways and to what extent academic research in politics and international studies (POLIS) has had impact, not exclusively in terms of official research assessment, but using that prism. In doing so, we also consider what, in terms of peer review and external evaluation of research, might characterise 'world-leading' research impact (issues discussed below).

The questions: impact in international affairs

The point about 'world-leading' research was a particular trigger for this study and the sense that, in the UK, politics and international studies, as a field, had relatively underperformed — all the more so, given the

---

18 See www.usip.org accessed at 29 July 2019.

19 The Wilson Center is distinct from most other major funders because its work is focused at the centre in DC, providing programme and open competitive opportunities for scholars and practitioners to work in complete academic freedom on subjects of their choice; but, in the nature of the Center and those who tend to seek to work there, scholars and fellows, generally work on topics of real world influence — most notably, around the time of writing, on US-China relations, following the opening of its Kissinger Institute. For a sense of the Wilson Center's range of global thematic and regional research, see www.wilsoncenter.org/research accessed at 29 July 2019.

20 Traditionally, the Harry Frank Guggenheim Foundation gave small grants for work on 'violence, aggression and dominance' with a completely open call and no expectation of anything beyond scholarly work — though it did have an interest in research making a difference in the world, evidenced, inter alia, by its support for what was summarised as 'the Freedman project' at King's College London, led by Gow, which sought to appreciate the nature of Professor Sir Lawrence Freedman's combination of scholarly and policy world success, with both Freedman and the Foundation 'committed to the aspiration to use the very best research possible on conflict and violence to work for a real and beneficial difference in the world.' James Gow and Benedict Wilkinson, 'Preface' in Benedict Wilkinson and James Gow, eds., *The Art of Creating Power: Freedman on Strategy*, London: Hurst/New York: OUP, 2017. For the Foundation itself, see www.hfg.org accessed at 29 July 2019.

original essence of that field, in the aftermath of the 1914–1919 War — or, even, before it, in terms of the 'politics' part and the mission of APSA, the American Political Science Association, in 1903. Already, in 2008, before 'impact' had emerged formally as a factor, one prominent scholar, who went on to become a very senior university figure and was already, at that point, in leading funding council roles, bemoaned the outcome of the national evaluation process, at that point called the RAE (Research Assessment Exercise), saying that the 'discipline had shot itself in the foot' — a view shared by many others at the annual convention of BISA, the British International Studies Association, the professional organisation for the field, after publication of the outcomes. This meant, in essence, that the peer review panel had been too mean, or too harsh, in its assessments, in relation to other subjects, where average outcomes were higher. Politics and International Studies lost out, given that these exercises determined the dispersal of Quality Research funding, so more money went to other areas. Whether this outcome was purely meanness on the part of that politics and international studies panel, or whether panels in other areas had simply been generous, the key point was that the approach of the panel had, overall, damaged the subject.

That trend continued in the renamed REF (Research Excellence Framework), in 2014. The research excellence exercise was conducted with four 'main panels' and various 'sub-panels' under their umbrellas. Universities (and cognate research organisations) submitted individual 'units of assessment' (UoA) to the relevant sub-panels. The main panels covered the broadest types of activity — although not actually labelled, the panels covered: A — Medicine; B — Science and Technology; C — Social Sciences; D — Arts and Humanities. Each of those main panels subsumed several units of assessment — of which, there were 36 in total — each with a sub-panel for evaluation of submissions. One of those 36 units was Politics and International Studies, Unit of Assessment 21, under Main Panel C.

While the discussions after 2008 might, or might not, have changed the approach of the newly constituted sub-panel, overall, in terms of its evaluation of research 'outputs' (publications), a degree of meanness appeared to be applied to the novel element in the exercise, 'impact.' As an unknown aspect of the exercise, no one could have a clear sense beforehand of that which might actually constitute 'world-leading' research.[21] Many, including senior figures at our own King's

---

21 Each university's submission to a particular unit of assessment was evaluated for originality, significance and rigour, against five possible ratings: Unclassified; 1*

College London, involved in some of the pre-REF discussions, believed that the top categories would only rarely be achieved.[22] With no benchmarks and past experience to guide, the 2014 results apparently confirmed this, with the outcome for impact seemingly about right, as some commentators judged.[23] Four universities had done very well, each gaining an average some way over 70 per cent 4*. A few others had done rather well, averaging scores in the 60s. This was not, perhaps, an unreasonable outcome, given the novelty of the exercise and the uncertainty surrounding it. But, it was also, surely a little underwhelming for a subject area with the idea of having impact at its very origin and core. This was reinforced when other UoAs' results were considered, which outperformed Politics and International Studies.

Reasons for any relative underperformance could be speculated. Impact was a new item on the agenda, so, perhaps, no one was ready for it. Yet, two factors bring this possible explanation into question. The first and most immediate is that, almost out of sight and unnoticed (see below), 111 impact case studies entered in that same REF exercise, spread across a range of subjects and disciplines in 35 submissions, all achieved the top 4* rating for the impact parts of the submission.[24] Secondly, as noted above, international studies was intended to make a difference and, especially, from the US, had been funded to do so, for example by the MacArthur Foundation. If anything, Politics and International Studies should have been in the forefront of successful research impact. In the end, this makes the relative failure a greater challenge to understand, which is the purpose of the book that follows.

That general sense of 'could have done better' might simply be reason to investigate further to see if that really might have been the case, in addition to the overall question of considering how well the academic field had performed over its first century. However, a stronger one is evidence that achieving 100 per cent 4* impact was possible, which accentuated the sense of politics and international

(One Star) — nationally recognised; 2* (Two Star) — internationally recognised; 3* (Three Star) — internationally excellent; and 4* (Four Star) — world-leading research. In terms of impact assessment, the descriptors were gauged in terms of reach and significance — see Chapter 5.

22 Thankfully, such judgements were misplaced and those of us who regarded work as likely to do well were closer to the mark — as those involved acknowledged ex post facto.

23 Christopher R. Moran and Christopher S. Browning, 'REF impact and the discipline of politics and international studies', *British Politics* Vol. 13 2018, pp. 249–69.

24 See Annex 1.

studies' underperformance. In July 2017, Dr. Steven Hill, then Director of Research Policy at the body responsible for the research excellence exercises,[25] made a presentation at an event organised by the TCCE (The Culture Capital Exchange) on research impact and the arts,[26] which Gow (already long-interested in matters of research impact) attended. Incidentally, one of Steven Hill's slides revealed something very interesting. An 'impact' submission in Unit of Assessment 35 had achieved 100 per cent world-leading impact, the maximum rating of 4* for the whole of its submission. This ran against all expectations and assumptions, such as those heard across the span of international studies and, as already mentioned, in senior circles at our own university, that complete success was unrealistic and unachievable. Performance in Politics and International Studies, on first look, appeared to confirm the same understanding, though high performance was clearly not impossible, as Oxford was rated 84 per cent 4* and a couple of others clearly in the 70s range. But, complete success, even for the most successful submissions, was assumed to be impossible. And yet, there, to be glimpsed in Steven Hill's presentation, was a case in the arts that gained a full score. That really cast a shadow on international affairs, a field in which research impact ought to be intrinsic. On further inspection, having broken the prejudice barrier that 100 per cent 4* would be impossible, and starting to looking around, more and more instances were found across various disciplines, and that shadow became longer and stronger.

The perfect outcomes in a range of other units of assessment prompted the sense that politics and international studies seemed to have underperformed — whether that reason was the self-harm to their field of panel members, as had been believed in 2008, or simply, that the accomplishments across the subject area had not been consistently world leading, at any institution. This posed serious questions about international studies. Why did the field of politics and international studies relatively underperform in terms of 'impact' in the UK

25 At that point, Steven Hill was Director of Research Policy at HEFCE — the Higher Education Funding Council for England, the body responsible for the REF (albeit that separate funding councils for the other constituent countries of the United Kingdom delivered the REF in their respective jurisdictions). Subsequently, he gained the new title of Director of Research, after reorganisation of research funding in the UK created a new overarching body, UKRI — UK Research and Innovation, and research in England became the responsibility of Research England.

26 Dr. Steven Hill, 'Developing Your Research Impact', *Hack-a-demia 2.0*, TCCE (The Capital Cultural Exchange), London, 10 July 2017.

Research Excellence Framework (REF) in 2014? Why did no submission in the unit of assessment gain a 100 per cent 4* — that is,
world-leading — impact rating? While previously this might have been
presumed to be because it was simply too difficult to achieve, as many
had assumed both before and after the 2014 exercise was conducted, there
was evidence from other disciplines that this presumption did not stand.

Were other subject areas better? Were the panels involved 'softer', or
more self-protective of their domains? Chiefly, what were the characteristics of those full-score submissions? Were there common features to them, and how might those features be related generally to the
understanding of impact, and, in particular, to impact in international
affairs? These are the questions with which we are concerned in the
remainder of the present volume, along with that initial enquiry: after
100 years, and given its *raison d'être*, to what extent has academic
research in international affairs had the real-world impact its founders
hoped to achieve?

Contexts

This is a distinctive and groundbreaking study. No book, or article,
has focused either on questions of impact in international affairs and
politics, or on the characteristics of 4* impact — world-leading impact.
The closest reference points, on impact, are the work by Mark Reed
and his colleagues at Newcastle University, and by Gemma Derrick at
Lancaster University, both discussed below. On the international affairs side, there is nothing comparable to that which we attempt in this
volume. From these statements, it is clear, however, that there are two
contexts for our analysis: international studies and research impact.
In the present section, we shall briefly address these contexts, better to
situate our research.

As noted already, the subject known as 'International Relations',
'International Affairs', 'International Politics' or 'International
Studies', marked its centenary in 2019. Many scholars use these terms
interchangeably, though distinction can operate between them. What
they all have in common is that they are concerned with matters that
cross the boundaries of states — where states are qualified by the
quality of 'sovereignty' (legally and politically) and mutual recognition
of that status,[27] and the terms 'nation' and 'state' are taken to be

---

27 'Sovereignty' — the fundamental concept in both international politics and inter-
    national law — concerns the supreme rights not to be told by outsiders what to do

synonyms.[28] 'Affairs' is probably the most open of these terms, though 'Studies' is also quite open, but limited to scholarly observation and evaluation, in some way. By contrast, 'international' 'affairs' might also embrace any form of practice that crosses borders, or is defined by the differences between actors on different sides of borders. It allows for anything connected with life between states and across their borders. 'International Politics' is the most narrow, in the more obvious senses, because it focuses on one area of activity — albeit one that can embrace many different aspects. But, it clearly sets boundaries that distinguish it from 'International Economics', or 'International Law.'

'International Relations' is the most common and possibly most problematic of these various terms, however. It is broad enough, intrinsically, to embrace international economics and international law, as well as any other matter crossing boundaries between states. This catholic version of international relations can often be better designated with lower case, to distinguish it from the version that is largely the focus of university departments teaching and researching the discipline titled International Relations, with capitals, often, to designate its status as a noun.[29] That version, while not excluding breadth, became largely focused on theory and a concomitant tussle between different ideological views, in essence, of politics and the international world. This struggle was in place, in effect, from the very start of the study of international relations. We sketch this in the following paragraphs.

Founded by Welsh and liberal politician David Davies, as already

within the given domain and to be able to decide on matters within that domain. States thus qualified are established by mutual recognition of possessing that qualification and enter into relations with one another in an international society, where, because of the nature of sovereignty, there is no overarching superior, as was indelibly captured in Hedley Bull, *The Anarchical Society: A Study of Order in World Politics*, London: Macmillan, 1977.

28 The term 'nation' has two distinct uses that reflect different ideas of being 'born together.' One stems from the French Revolution and distinguishes 'people', generally, from the 'nation', those who belong together in a state. The other version concerns those born together in blood, irrespective of state-territorial circumstances, sharing common symbols and practices. See, for example, James Mayall, *Nationalism and International Society*, Cambridge Studies in International Relations: 10, Cambridge: Cambridge University Press, 1990.

29 There are many useful introductions to international relations; for those seeking a general guide, the following can be useful, as a fairly modern and comprehensive approach: John Baylis, Steve Smith and Patricia Owens, eds., *The Globalization of World Politics: An introduction to international relations*, 6th ed., Oxford: Oxford University Press, 2014.

noted, in 1919, at the University of Wales, Aberystwyth, the impetus was very much to focus on peace and, with the First World War only just finishing, to conduct research on how to prevent war — indeed, with a legal aspect, to outlaw it.[30] However, the fourth incumbent of that chair, E.H. Carr, a great historian, especially of the Russian Revolution and the Soviet Union, developed a perspective on the years between the two world wars, captured in his seminal, *The Twenty Years Crisis, 1919–1939*, that brought into question what he termed 'idealism' — the thinking, by those such as David Davies, that hoped to eradicate war in favour of peace, arguing effectively that it was misguided and misplaced. Instead, Carr urged the need for 'realism' — by which, he meant a focus on being realistic, on being pragmatic and on the empirical necessity of dealing with those who did not share the same 'idealist' visions for the world.[31]

That tension between 'idealism' and 'realism' permeated the study of International Relations subsequently. In contrast to Carr's 'realism' as a call for a sober sense of empirical reality, an ideological, theoretical interpretation of realism emerged. This views the world, and international politics, in particular, in terms of material self-interest and benefit, where rational actors focus on the maximisation of power to achieve, above all else, security — that is, the security of the state, in a world defined by states in an insecure, anarchical set of relationships with each other.[32] International studies came to be dominated by

---

30 The University of Wales, Aberystwyth, later to be Aberystwyth University in its own right, continued to become one of the leading places in the world for the study of International Relations. David Davies's own role was recognised with the creation of the David Davies Memorial Centre, which focused on research on diplomacy, peace and security and human rights, and its journal, *International Relations*, became one of the prominent publications in the field; originally, the Centre was based in London, close to Parliament and reflecting its political roots, but, at a point of generational change, and with an appropriate sense of harmonisation, it was relocated to be hosted by Aberystwyth.

31 E. H. Carr, *The Twenty Years Crisis, 1919–1939: The Politics of Power and Security*, London: Macmillan, 1951 (originally, 1939).

32 The father of political realism was Hans J. Morgenthau, whose work is far richer and more subtle than many assume, or give credit for — indeed, the full interpretation of Morgenthau as, in effect, a Constructivist remains to be made, although Ned Lebow has made a creditable start. See Hans J. Morgenthau, *Politics Among Nations: The Struggle for Power and Peace*, brief edition, New York: McGraw-Hill, 1993; Richard Ned Lebow, *The Tragic Vision of Politics: Ethics, Interests and Orders*, Cambridge University Press, 2003; other major figures succeeding Morgenthau include Kenneth N. Waltz, *Theory of International Politics*, Reading, MA: Addison Wesley, 1979, and John Mearsheimer, *The Tragedy of Great Power Politics*, New York: Norton, 2001.

theoretical debates between this realism and various opposing perspectives — idealism, liberalism (or liberal institutionalism),[33] English School thought, socialism, Marxism, 'critical' perspectives,[34] and also 'constructivist' approaches — although these are sometimes, as with Alexander Wendt's innovative introduction of the term, simply seeking to be contenders to the crown of political realism,[35] rather than using the full potential of the approach.[36] Americans dominated these theoretical debates, simply because of the scale of the academic market there and the quality of its institutions, but the English School 'international society', cosmopolitan and critical approaches are important in other parts of the world.

While these theoretical arguments were driven by differing worldviews and interpretations of how policy in the real world should be founded and directed, for the most part, the scope of this academic discourse held little relevance for practitioners. Historically, the ISA — the International Studies Association — was formed in the US in 1959 to provide a forum in which scholars and policy practitioners could come together. The scope of this organisation extends beyond theoretical debates, with sections on topics such as diplomacy, communication, security, development, law and so on.[37] Yet, theoretical disputes continued to dominate and impact remained limited — indeed, being rejected as the notion of 'professionalism' grew in the 1970s. This limited impact is surprising given the origins of the discipline, already noted.

33 For a limited number of surveys of the variety of views encompassed by Liberalism, Idealism and their variants see, for example: Michael P. Doyle, *Ways of War and Peace: Realism, Liberalism, and Socialism*, New York: W.W. Norton and Co., 1997; Joshua S. Goldstein, *International Relations*, 3rd ed., New York: Longman, 1999, ch. 3; Tim Dunne, 'Liberalism' in John Baylis and Steve Smith, *The Globalization of World Politics: An Introduction to International Relations*, Oxford University Press, 2001; Scott Burchill, 'Liberalism' in Scott Burchill *et al.*, *Theories of International Relations*, 2nd ed., London: Palgrave, 2001.

34 See Burchill *et al.*, *Theories of International Relations*, and Steve Smith, Ken Booth and Marysia Zalewski, eds., *International Theory: Positivism and Beyond*, Cambridge University Press, 1996.

35 Alexander Wendt, *The Social Theory of International Relations*, Cambridge University Press, 1999, p.xiii; see also, Wendt, 'Anarchy is What States Make It: The Social Construction of Power Politics', *International Organization* Vol. 46 No. 2 1992; and Smith, 'Reflectivist and Constructivist Approaches to International Theory' in Baylis and Smith, eds, *Globalization*, ch. 11.

36 James Gow, 'Constructivist Realism and Necessity' in Wilkinson and Gow, eds., *The Art of Creating Power*.

37 For the full scope see www.isanet.org, accessed at 29 November 2019.

When actual research did make a difference, occasionally, it was where the policy makers were caught off guard and did not have understanding and policy in place, and required knowledge and understanding, in a hurry.[38] When called upon, that knowledge and understanding was usually highly empirical, whether biomedical assistance on Bird Flu in the 2000s, or detailed area studies knowledge, for example, of the Yugoslav lands, in the early 1990s. With the possible exception of Lawrence Freedman's *The Future of War: a History*, which indicated just how wrong many research projections turned out to be with reference to war, there has been no attempt, so far, by international affairs scholars, despite the origins of the field, to consider the extent to which research has made a difference in the world. The present study will be the first contribution in that context, as such.

The other context for the book is that of research impact. This has been a slowly emerging field, evolving from older notions of knowledge exchange, or knowledge transfer. While we devote Chapter 2 to discussing the notion of impact, it is relevant to note, at this point, the ways in which our research relates to — and significantly differs from — the small amount of work by others that does, none the less, provide some context for this book. First, the pioneers of research relating to impact, who did not necessarily use that term, focused more on the problems of understanding the distinction between dissemination of research and whether research actually made any difference. As early as 1980, Knott and Wildavsky had identified the 'dissemination problem' and sought to illustrate the important gap between presenting research findings and any actual and identified implementation of that research.[39] Similarly, as the amoebae of the impact agenda were incubating in the first decade of the 21st century, Sandra Nutley and colleagues pursued something of that same agenda, identifying the limitations of 'knowledge transfer' in the health sector, in particular, and seeking to push beyond them, chiming with calls for 'evidence-based policy' around the time of the first government of Prime Minister Tony Blair, in the UK.[40] These were pioneering studies, but they did not address the evaluation of excellent research.

38 Sir David Omand, 'Observations on Whitehall and Academia', in Wilkinson and Gow, eds., *The Art of Creating Power*.
39 J. Knott and A. Wildavsky, 'If dissemination is the solution, what is the problem?' *Knowledge: Creation, Diffusion, Utilization* Vol. 1, No. 4 1980.
40 Sandra M. Nutley, Isabel Walter and Huw Davies, *Using Evidence: How Research*

Three studies, in the wake of the UK REF exercise, where 'impact' was introduced formally as an element of evaluation, for the first time, did begin to address that evaluation agenda. The first of these was a study by Jonathan Grant and the Policy Institute at King's College London, commissioned by HEFCE, the body responsible for the REF evaluation.[41] As a first cut on the innovation of impact evaluation in REF2014, Grant and his team harvested 6,247,292 words from the 'details of impact' section of 6,679 publicly available case studies submitted as part of the exercise (some case studies were confidential and not publicly available). Using a blend of text-data mining and qualitative reading of a selection of 1,000 of the case studies (guided by the research), this study identified 60 impact topics, 3,709 discrete 'pathways to impact' and a range of beneficiaries of research around the world. However, aside from noting the use of numbers in case studies, as support (which use was so varied and specific to cases as not to be comparable), the study made no attempt to gauge the characteristics of studies and provided no evaluation of the relative quality of the cases.

Mark Reed and his colleagues, at Newcastle University (and also Sheffield, Leeds and Northumbria), have done most to consider the evaluative outcome of REF2014 impact case studies (ICSs). This continuing research (as we write) produced articles,[42] as well as Reed's spin-off research and training company, Fast Track Impact, with its website (fasttrackimpact.com), offering guidance on 'how to achieve 4* impact.' This research has focused on discourse analysis of high-scoring and low-scoring ICSs in REF2014 — the kind of language used and the actions it describes, and the way this use of language correlates to higher, or lower, rated case studies. The focus on pathways is useful and can guide understanding of both the

Can Inform Public Services, Bristol: Policy Press, 2007; and Huw Davies, Sandra Nutley and Isabel Walter, 'Why "knowledge transfer" is misconceived for applied social research', *Journal of Health Services Research & Policy* Vol. 13 No. 3 2008.

41 King's College London and Digital Science, *The nature, scale and beneficiaries of research impact: An initial analysis of Research Excellence Framework (REF) 2014 impact case studies*, Research Report 2015/01, Prepared for the Higher Education Funding Council of England, Higher Education Funding Council for Wales, Scottish Funding Council, Department of Employment and Learning Northern Ireland, Research Councils UK and the Wellcome Trust, London: HEFCE, 2015.

42 Bella Reichard, Mark S. Reed, Jenn Chubb, Ged Hall, Lucy Jowett and Alisha Peart, 'Pathways to a top-scoring impact case study', *Palgrave Communications* (in press at the time of writing).

presentation of impact and also, likely (though not clearly established) its substance, as language is likely to reflect substance, in such an exercise. However, despite the references to '4*', or 'world-leading' impact, it is evident that the research does not distinguish between that level and the 3* one below it, and so does not address the top level, *per se*. Nor, aside from the generic sense of use of active and concrete language over more passive and vague language, does this valuable work consider the characteristics that represent quality achievement in impact.

Finally, Gemma Derrick's landmark book *The Evaluator's Eye*,[43] is a pathbreaking study of how peer and lay reviewers carried out their roles in Main Panel A (medical, health, biological, agricultural, veterinary and food sciences) for REF2014. This is a remarkable piece of social research that offers excellent insight on how panel members approached their work and interpreted issues of impact and assessment, including the ways in which group dynamics quickly led to shared understandings of that which would represent levels of achievement and particular characteristics accompanying those levels. However, while an excellent and valuable study, it does not address the elements that characterise research impact judged to represent evidence of quality, nor, crucially, is there analysis of what actually was evaluated as 4*, world-leading research — not, of course, Derrick's purpose, which was to focus on the social processes and issues involved in peer evaluation.

It is evident that no study of impact has either identified what constitutes highest-level, world-leading research impact, in relation to the UK research excellence exercises, or independently of it. Nor has any study on impact focused systematically on international studies — just as nothing in the realm of international affairs, until this book, has analysed the difference that research makes. Just one initiative considered the impact issue in the context of Politics and International Studies — a special issue of *British Politics*.[44] For the most part, the diverse articles in the collection considered issues of impact, mainly the various difficulties surrounding it, albeit linked to the field, both broadly and in niche contexts, such as intelligence studies.[45] Just two

43 Derrick, *The Evaluator's Eye*.
44 'Special Issue: The Impact Agenda in British Higher Education', *British Politics* Vol. 13 No. 3 September 2018.
45 Robert Dover and Michael S. Goodman, 'Impactful scholarship in intelligence: a public policy challenge', *British Politics* Vol. 13 2018, pp. 374–91.

of the articles provide assessment of the impact achieved by the field. One is the excellent survey introduction by Christophers Moran and Browning, which discusses the relative performance of the field in the first REF impact exercise, judging it to be reasonable, given the tangle of inherent problems they identify. However, they do this despite identifying the same mission to make a difference that we highlight above. Rather than gauging against the expectations that mission might create, or the correlation between that mission and outcomes achieved, instead, they interpret results against the entangling triffids they see as limiting the field's scope for impact.[46] The only article that examines impact in international studies specifically is devoted to noting that none of 43 cases studies it considers from 'top' submissions reflected a 'critical' perspective.[47] Although the article shares several of our observations about some scholars' resistance to engagement and the unsuitability of some approaches to making a difference, and urges a different approach, its core position is limited to identifying the absence of 'critical' research, rather than considering the character and quality of that which is there. None of this investigates impact itself in the field.

That investigation is our mission. The book is novel as a study of impact in international relations, as an analysis of international studies in terms of impact research, and unique, in any sense, in its inquiry into, and identification of, the characteristics of world-leading, highest-calibre research's making a difference in the world, following the REF process. As such, we believe that it will be of value and interest to those working in each of these fields, as well as to many others, including those interested as what are often labelled 'beneficiaries' and those tackling the issues of research impact and presenting it for evaluation purposes, in the UK and around the world.

Scope and methodology

The present study forms part of a continuing programme of activity evaluating and investigating the evaluation of the impact of academic research. That activity began around 2010, as 'impact' began to permeate discourse of research funders and assessors, in the UK, in

46 Moran and Browning, 'REF impact and the discipline of politics and international studies'
47 Jan Selby, 'Critical international relations and the impact agenda', *British Politics* Vol. 13 2018, pp. 332–47.

particular. That addition to the lexicon spread quickly, both in the British context and internationally, infiltrating every discipline, or field of academic inquiry. It certainly ran through our own focus of research on security, conflict and justice, and the broader contexts of politics and international studies, in which we work. This study covers relevant research in those domains, but also, in our quest to understand the characteristics of quality and a perceived under-performance in politics and international studies, reflecting the universal in university, it stretches across the galaxy of research. The aim of the study is to evaluate impact in international affairs, in the round, in an attempt to understand the seemingly weaker-than-could-be-expected performance of politics and international studies in the formal UK septennial research accountability and evaluation exercise, in 2014. It does not focus on 2014, but builds a picture in relation to research activity and findings, and knowledge generated, in the past, over a longer timeframe. In particular, this investigation, to assist in research selection, considers investments made by funders, especially the UK research councils in the 21st century, such as the pathbreaking series of 'New Security Challenges' programmes directed by Stuart Croft, within the realm of international affairs and security, broadly. This, inevitably, is an exercise that lacks precision and involves an element of chance — identifying funded research, in the first instance, and then selecting within that collection research that relates to our field. The study we present includes analysis of research and research funding, and impact activity and potential, on this basis; but, we recognise that there are limitations to our study and that, aside from the need to be compact for a volume, such as this, there might well be gaps in our approach that have eluded us. None the less, we judge that the research and our findings hold value, despite any such lacunae.

The research covered by this study includes projects funded solely by one funder, or in collaboration with others. In particular, we consider research funded by bodies such as the ESRC, the AHRC, DFID, the MoD and DSTL, and the FCO,[48] in the UK — the first two, research councils, the rest government departments that significantly fund, or co-fund, international-focused research. We also consider research

---

48 These acronyms are for: the Economic and Social Research Council; the Arts and Humanities Research Council; the Department for International Development; the Ministry of Defence; the Defence Science and Technology Laboratory; and the Foreign and Commonwealth Office.

underpinned by funding from major international sources, notably US foundations, such as Ford and MacArthur. There are two reasons for this. First, it reflects a general global trend to conduct interdisciplinary and interagency research, requiring activity that 'in partnership with other stakeholders' would produce 'a portfolio of high impact, inter-disciplinary research contributing to UK security objectives', in the terms of one research funder.[49] Secondly, it facilitates our inquiry. It is not possible to examine each research project ever funded in detail — let alone those conducted without external support. Therefore it makes sense to target investigation on major investments, such as programmes co-funded by the ESRC, the AHRC, DFID, DSTL and the FCO, in particular, which gave a directed focus for relevant research. A critical mass of funding and research, therefore, was formed by these programmes and their projects — or 'investments' as the funders would term them. This emphasis is not, however, to the exclusion entirely of other research. But it does reflect economy of engagement, given the potential volume of material and the scope of our study. Beyond this, as described a little more fully in Chapter 4, for our evaluation of REF impact case studies, we have relied on the publicly available information and sets of studies as presented by REF2014, identifying both outcomes in relation to international studies and, crucially, those across the full spectrum of REF submissions, where achievement of the top-level, 'world-leading' '4*' (Four Star) evaluation was achieved.

The process of selecting material to investigate is one part of the mixed methodology adopted for the study. The variety of methods used all constitute qualitative research (aside from simple arithmetical processes, such as categorisation of projects, or counting of case studies, or processing numbers found in the research). Assessment of social science research impact — including identification of impact itself — is a problematic area, discussed later, throughout the book, but especially in Chapter 2. The use of quantitative approaches, especially to gauge 'economic impact', is particularly, if not completely prohibitively, one aspect of the difficulty. As one study for the ESRC noted, 'economic evaluations are only relevant in certain circum-stances' and even then 'should be applied in the context of broader qualitative assessments.'[50] The principal method adopted was

---

49 *ESRC Strategic Plan 2009–14: Delivering Impact Through Social Science*, Swindon: ESRC, No Date.
50 *Taking Stock: A Summary of ESRC's Work to Evaluate the Impact of Research on Policy and Practice,* No Place: ESRC, February 2009, p. 18.

empirical, critical evaluation of documents for all aspects of the research. The range of documentation included: a selection of material from REF and Research Councils; reports by researchers on projects, where available; publications and other forms of output; and official documents. In the course of our research, overall, but not for this particular study, we conducted informal consultations with a small selection of relevant people, informal conversations and informal interviews;[51] these were conducted over many years, however, and not for the purpose of this study. We mention them because, inevitably, these contacts inform the research in some ways, as part of our context and culture — we cannot undo our knowledge and understanding. But, they are not used directly and do not contribute substantially to the work here. In a similar vein, lesser aspects of research included observation and participation while attending events — actions and perception that help form our understanding, and which we cannot 'unlearn' or distinguish from the general understanding we have developed. In addition, internet searches were used, which did not merely identify documents, although this was surely the main achievement, but also undoubtedly influenced us through passing 'chatter' and discussion. In one part of our research, based in the School of Security Studies at King's, we used a questionnaire, but the responses to this aspect of the research were limited and make no necessary contribution to the research presented, although we, again, cannot exclude some influence for that overall process. That said, we must declare strongly that only the process of interview could bring out the most relevant material, when seeking to identify impact with investigators — questionnaires elicit only data of very limited value, in that context. However, as the purpose in this project is not to tease out examples of research impact (a key activity that we undertook as part of our overall research project), but to examine top-level research impact and impact evaluation, no research interviews substantively or directly inform the study presented here, although we have used these in another context.[52]

---

51 Interviews involved a mixture of informal consultations, interpretive biographical and semi-structured approaches.

52 We would not be surprised if our experience in using questionnaires were shared by others, finding them disappointing and sometimes complicating already difficult judgements; nor would it be surprising if others found that interviews helped significantly in making those sorts of judgements.

The book

This introduction has established the contexts for this study and posed a series of questions. These include the initial and overarching challenge: after reaching 100, to what extent did international studies fulfil a founding purpose to make a difference in the world? They also include the crucial, more focused and refined version of that question: to what extent, as it seems *prima facie*, did the field of politics and international studies relatively underperform in terms of 'impact' in the UK Research Excellence Framework (REF) in 2014? Why did no submission gain a 100 per cent 4* — that is, world-leading — impact rating? And, we can add, if there was underperformance, why was this the case? The initial mission of international relations, much in the scope of research funding to the area, and the demands of evaluation exercises, all make the relative failure of the field a challenge to understand. That is the purpose of the book that follows, having posed the challenge in this first chapter.

In Chapter 2, we examine the notion of 'impact' itself. As impact has become a 'trend' in academic and policy discussions, establishing that which constitutes 'impact' has become a challenge in different contexts. There are small, perhaps subtle, differences in use of the term 'impact' between different organisations. Impact can mean the 'influence' of research or its 'effect on' an individual, a community, the development of policy, or the creation of a new product or service. It relates to the effects of research on our economic, social and cultural lives. The degree to which a change must be beneficial is, of course, debatable — especially as benefit can clearly be in the eyes of both beholders and those affected (or not). In any case, conventionally, as we set out in Chapter 3, impact can occur in four types: conceptual, instrumental, capacity building and procedural. This typology informs the remainder of the book.

Having established an understanding of research impact and its types, in Chapter 4 we present a brief historical overview of impact in the field of international affairs. First, the chapter considers the impact question in international perspective, particularly, though not exclusively, with reference to the United States and funders providing the resources to support research and researchers focused on making differences in societies, practice and policy, in the US and globally. The second section analyses the 'impact' of British international and security research before the advent of the official institutional impact agenda. This research finds that things were uneven with a few striking successes, indicating some potential for world-leading outcomes in REF2014, but also disappointment and a general sense that impact had been underwhelming. In the final section, the top outcomes in Politics and International Studies in REF2014, all somewhere short of the 100 per cent 4* levels, are discussed. The review reinforces the sense that in REF2014, Politics and International Studies underperformed.

Having reviewed the scope of research impact in international affairs and questioned performance of the sector in the UK REF exercise, we turn to the question of identifying 'world-leading' research, in terms of that exercise. We do so in two ways. First, in Chapter 5, before presenting our own research, we give a critical exposition of pathfinding, insightful research on language and discourse in high-scoring (3* and 4*) ICSs in REF2014, led by Mark Reed and his Fast Track Impact team. Although this analysis does not isolate 4* ICSs and would be insufficient as a template, it provides valuable evidence of how to achieve 4* research impact, which is complementary to our own understanding, but completely different in nature and findings. Our analysis is presented in Chapters 6 and 7. The chapters present the results from a study of 111 4* ICSs from REF2014 known certainly to have achieved the highest level. The chapters entail a unique analysis of 'world-leading' (4*) research in REF2014. We judge that the consistency of features identified gives a reliable foundation for understanding what constitutes a 4* ICS. After consideration of all 111 ICSs that were judged to be 4*, 'world leading' in 2014, we conclude that eight elements are common to known 4* research ICSs: 1. long-term research and impact context; 2. quality/ significant research funding; 3. clear engagement/an embedded role in implementation/researcher-practitioner unity; 4. resource/financial commitment to impact; 5. quotes as evidence and presentation; 6. breadth/range/multiplicity/cumulative effect; 7. creating something new/transformative for beneficiaries; 8. news media engagement and public engagement. These are presented with examples in the course of the two chapters, with the first five covered in Chapter 6 and the remainder in Chapter 7.

Finally, in the Conclusion, we review the analysis presented as a whole. In the final chapter, we return to the question of the relative failure of Politics and International Studies in REF2014, in light of the analysis of 4* ICSs in Chapters 5–7. First, we review issues of impact and the typology introduced, including the innovative procedural impact and the significance of media and public engagement that may constitute a fourth type of impact, alongside the triad of conceptual, instrumental and capacity building identified in Chapter 2. In the second section, we summarise that which constitutes 'world-leading' research impact and indicate the eight characteristics in the quest for 4*s, along with reflection on our research findings. In the final section we address 'why POLIS fails', considering the nature of the subject and forms of knowledge, as well as what might be a relative 'mean spiritedness' about the field in the past, where the discipline has been said to 'shoot itself in the foot.'

2   Impact — concept and issues

King's College London, where we researched for and wrote this book, has a mission historically to conduct research and develop 'knowledge in the service of society.' This is not, perhaps, truly, the antithesis of an 'ivory tower' approach to the academy, involving the purity of research entirely for its own sake and the good of knowledge itself, as it respects and embraces that alternative mission and eschews a purely utilitarian approach. Yet, it is, from the purist perspective, unacceptable and sinful. There is a tension between the pluralist embrace of research for its own sake alongside openness to making a difference in the world through the development of knowledge (and even the determined desire actively to make such a difference), on one side, and the untainted quest for knowledge for its own sake, on the other.

To some, the purity of the academic enterprise is sacred and not to be tainted by contact with the 'real' world. To others, the mission to seek to make a difference through research is second nature.[1] While each of these positions creates a pole, the reality is that much in the realm of academic research has always had 'impact', in that it has made a difference in the world — from philosophies of liberalism, through to the identification of medicines and therapies. The problem, so far as it clearly existed, was that the specific and institutional identification of the term 'impact' and its labelling was new to the academic context and appeared to be an additional expectation and

---

1 This opposition was evident when one young Dutch researcher used one of the authors, Gow, as an informant in her research into the 'problem' of academics engaging with international criminal tribunals. She was clearly thoroughly imbued with the purity of the ivory tower and reacted with complete astonishment to the suggestion that, in line with the King's mission statement and most medical research, for example, engagement of the kind in question could be seen as a matter of academic — and social — responsibility.

burden. Moreover, this addition was not only something seemingly 'extra', but it was also, it felt to some, contrary to the scholarly mission to pursue knowledge for its own sake and, in the tradition of academic tenure, to be the guardians of knowledge and its free, unfettered and un-pressured development.[2]

Against this background, in the present chapter, we explore the idea of impact, its meaning and some of the issues and debates surrounding it. The study has, inevitably, involved critical reflection on the concept of impact and its evaluation. This is introduced and discussed here, and informs the remainder of the book theoretically. First, however, we consider the matter of defining impact and the questions that surround attempts to focus it beyond the broad sense of 'making a difference' that we have used so far — a sense that will, none the less, also continue to have bearing throughout the book.

Defining impact

As impact became a 'trend' in academic and policy discussions, so, establishing that which constitutes 'impact' became a challenge in different contexts. This study focuses on institutionally conceived and understood impact, for example by research councils, such as the ESRC (Economic and Social Research Council) looking for 'value' in its 'investments', or the concern of most British academics, focused on the UKRI (UK Research and Innovation) and national research bodies (or associated) approaches to 'impact' for the Research Excellence Framework (REF). As the notion emerged and developed, there were small, perhaps subtle, differences in use of the term 'impact' between different bodies in their documentation, reflecting evolving usage and, perhaps, for some time, slightly different priorities. These are discussed in the current section, which sets out definitional discussions, on the road to more settled and coherent usage of the term.

The initial HEFCE (Higher Education Funding Council for England — the predecessor of Research England, currently responsible for REF in England) definition of 'impact as any identifiable benefit to or positive influence on the economy, society, public policy or services,

---

2 Recognising this traditional image of scholarly endeavour is not, we would stress, to view that image as unproblematic. Both this image and that of the researcher making a difference, as well as any other variants, rest on questions of values in knowledge formation and issues of epistemology, which questions inform the enquiry of certain researchers.

culture, the environment or quality of life',[3] was considerably more open than many others. Indeed, it was apparently broader than the subsequent clarification that 'inputs' were distinct from 'impact':

> For example, providing advice to a policy committee is considered an 'input'. A change to government policy, influenced by that advice, is considered an 'interim impact.'[4]

The latter was largely consistent with the definition offered in ESRC documentation, around the same time:

> [D]issemination is not impact: impact evaluation of social science research should therefore look beyond dissemination to capture evidence of application by research users.[5]

However, the former was broader, rightly going beyond the ESRC's pairing of 'policy and practice.'[6] This broadening was also reflected in the description-cum-definition of impact attributed to the then-Research Councils UK (RCUK), generally, as they sought to offer a joint and common view of the topic:

> The Research Councils describe impact as the demonstrable contribution that excellent research makes to society and the economy. Impact embraces all the extremely diverse ways in which research-related knowledge and skills benefit individuals, organisations and nations by:
>
> • fostering global economic performance, and specifically the economic competitiveness of the United Kingdom

---

3 It is important to note the 'positive' value evident in this definition. However, impact need not necessarily be 'positive', even if as noted, for example, by the authors of one ESRC study (*Taking Stock: A Summary of ESRC's Work to Evaluate the Impact of Research on Policy and Practice*, ESRC, February 2009), it is evidence of the positive version of impact that HEFCE — and other bodies — seek to identify, in responding to government agendas and demands for 'evidence' of value and use. The biased definition of impact is briefly discussed below.

4 *Research Excellence Framework impact pilot exercise: Findings of the expert panels: A report to the UK higher education funding bodies by the chairs of the impact pilot panels*, Higher Education Funding Council for England, November 2010.

5 ESRC, *Taking Stock*.

6 ESRC, *Taking Stock*.

- increasing the effectiveness of public services and policy; and
- enhancing quality of life, health and creative output.

Impact can mean the 'influence' of research or its 'effect on' an individual, a community, the development of policy, or the creation of a new product or service. It relates to the effects of research on our economic, social and cultural lives.[7]

There could be judged to be elements of confusion or uncertainty in this statement of impact. The three bullet points were considerably narrower in several respects — the seeming focus on economics, business, policy and the UK — than the broader terms in the concluding paragraph, where the use of 'influence' in quotation marks offered a far wider range of potential effects, as did the suggestion that individuals and communities were relevant. The last paragraph also allowed the life, health and creative aspects of the third bullet point, brief as they were, not completely to be lost, as they easily could have been.

The use of 'application' to define impact in some ESRC literature, at one point, appeared to be a stronger requirement than either the HEFCE or RCUK definitions demanded.[8] This standard of 'impact' was, perhaps, close to that of Knott and Wildavsky, for whom 'impact' stands at the top of a seven-point scale and refers only to the identifiable and measurable success of a policy (or practice, or product, or similar), which is fully implemented and based on original research.[9] In this sense, impact is only achieved when research has, in their terms, provided evidence for policy, which policy, when fully implemented, can be tangibly gauged to have been successful. In practice, in most areas, this level of impact is unlikely to be achieved and it is probably unreasonable to discuss this as 'impact' in anything other than theoretical terms. In practice, studies show that, even if 'application' could be stretched to reflect levels 5 and 6 of the Knott and Wildavsky impact ladder (adoption and implementation, respectively), this would clearly leave other aspects worth noting as impact out of the frame

---

7 *Details of the call for proposals to the Beyond Text: Performances, Sounds, Images, Objects Programme Follow on Funding Scheme*, AHRC, October 2010.

8 As discussed in the remainder of this paragraph, 'application', as a notion, lies at the highest ranks of 'impact', while 'effects' and similar terms used in other definitions can be correlated to lower levels of research use.

9 J. Knott and A. Wildavsky, 'If dissemination is the solution, what is the problem?' *Knowledge: Creation, Diffusion, Utilization* Vol. 1, No. 4, 1980.

(for example, cognition and contributions to conceptualisation and development of policy and practices). Most 'impact' falls well short of even this level of 'instrumentality', with what has been described as 'enlightenment' constituting the most common outcome — activity which might only correlate to steps 1 and 2 in the Knott and Wildavsky chain.[10] This is significant, as a major Canadian study on impact shows that perhaps one in six projects has any impact at all — 16 per cent.[11] This is one of the most developed studies of impact undertaken. It is based on a corrected sample of 1,288 questionnaire respondents with at least a 20-year perspective (the authors do not specify a time frame, per se, but note that the research developed against a background of two decades of increasing 'pressure to increase utilization [original] of university research').[12] As noted, implicitly and explicitly, in various ESRC documents, 'application' understood even in the broadest of these terms, might be impossible to achieve, or at least to confirm with evidence, because of the difficulties not only of seeing research translated directly into application, but also of identifying the processes by which this occurs, when it does.

In this context, the introduction of 'influencing' in the RCUK definition might be a term with greater utility. Yet, that term is also problematic, largely for the same reasons. Indeed, while 'application' might be observed empirically, 'influence' will be subject to explanation and interpretation by those involved, at best. In addition, the three bullet-point descriptors tend towards longer-term aims and processes, rather than objectives that could correlate to describable impact. However, they may be useful in indicating areas and activities in which impact might be identified empirically, although the final sentence is a succinct definition of impact ('effects on economic, social and cultural lives').

Yet, the HEFCE definition quoted above, with more named elements, remains stronger. 'Effects', as used in this RCUK definition, constitutes something perhaps both broader and intellectually more open than 'identifiable benefits' and 'positive effects', which are sought in the HEFCE definition noted above, and which broadly inform the present study. Effects may be negative, if not qualified. The use of

10 S. Sunesson and K. Nilsson, 'Explaining Research Utilization: beyond "functions"', *Knowledge: Creation, Diffusion, Utilization* Vol. 10, No. 2, 1988.
11 R. Landry, N. Amara and M. Lamari, 'Climbing the Ladder of Research Utilization', *Science Communication* Vol. 22, No. 4, 2001.
12 Landry *et al.*, 'Climbing the Ladder'.

'impact' only to refer to positive phenomena is clearly far from value neutral. There is an assumption by all concerned generally that impact is, and should be, positive. It is this positive, useful sense of impact that those involved in research, whether the researchers themselves or those who fund research, wish to demonstrate to those who provide the money. Likewise, it is evidence of this positive effect of money spent via research processes and of findings for which funders, notably the UK government, might look.[13]

It is important, of course, as well, to note that 'impact' is not necessarily a positive factor and does not necessarily mean value, or 'worth'. Indeed, what constitutes 'positive' may be contested, or might change over time, in light of changing perspectives (for example, the perceived benefit of single-use plastic bottles was transformed into a global crisis in 2016). It might be hard to determine definitively, or objectively. Moreover, there are some instances where whilst impact has been clearly significant, it has also had what could be considered as a disastrous impact. For example, the 'research' of Dr. Andrew Wakefield on links between the MMR vaccine and autism had great impact, in terms of gaining attention and significantly reducing uptake of the vaccine. However, the resurgence of the diseases was another, more important and certainly negative effect, while the research was roundly discredited and should not be conflated with genuine, beneficial impact (even if 'benefit' might well be a problematic term, at times).[14] Wakefield's research is an example of phenomenal impact, albeit of a disturbing and damaging kind. This is something that is not restricted to the medical field and can occur in unintended ways — one person's benefit may well be another's deficit.[15]

The negative aspects of impact should not be overlooked, and 'effects', therefore, constitutes an intellectually more honest element in the definition of impact. None the less, the value-biased HEFCE definition discussed retains its importance and, in many respects, remains the one that most informs the present study, as it is also this

13 ESRC, *Taking Stock*. Of course, others might have different perspectives on utility and its character.
14 Sandra M. Nutley, Isabel Walter and Huw T.O. Davies, *Using Evidence: How Research Can Inform Public Services*, Bristol: Policy Press, 2007, p. 295.
15 In the domain of international affairs, there is the theoretical possibility that research impact might mean preventing an incident, or process, from happening. However, the counterfactual problem of presenting this form of impact would be considerable, as there would be a need to prove and evaluate (or even measure) a non-event or non-process.

'loaded' understanding of the concept that, in practice, informs most interest and activity focused on impact. So long as both this general bias is consciously acknowledged by investigators and assessors, and evidence of arguably negative effect is not excluded, a focus on beneficial impact within the definition makes sense, as it reflects the broad character and purpose of attempts to gauge impact.

An institutionally more settled definition emerged on the path to REF2014. Following consideration of international approaches and a pilot REF exercise in the UK, HEFCE produced a broad and, for most observers, relatively comfortable version of the concept for official purposes. In this, impact was: 'an effect on, change, or benefit to the economy, society, culture, public policy or services, health, the environment or quality of life, beyond academia.'[16] While identifying specific objects of impact, the definition seemingly left open broad possibilities for interpretation both by those who make submissions and also those who would have to evaluate those submissions. This scope was, perhaps, to palliate the challenge of dealing with this new evaluative demand, allowing flexible approaches, so long as there was something 'beyond academia' that had been affected, or changed, by, or benefited from, excellent research. Moreover, 'effect', in itself, offered more possibilities for interpretation, even, than either 'change', or 'benefit', which latter two were clearly more potentially concrete and also, quite probably, more in the forefront of impact considerations. None the less, the relative openness of the REF2014 definition could also, still, be seen (and felt) as narrow and seeming to demand a particular kind of impact — an issue discussed further, below.

A decade on from the first real signs of institutional and official concern about impact, the official sense of what it was and how it should be understood became more settled. It was still subject to discussion — and, it seems, large numbers of academics in UK universities (probably an overwhelming majority) remained somewhat mystified, unclear, in the dark and anxious about the matter.[17] Before the various UK funding bodies, both the higher education funding

---

16 HEFCE, *Assessment Framework and guidance on submissions. REF 2014*, London: HEFCE, 2011.

17 So far as we are aware, there has been no substantial, or national, research on this question. However, from our own research and experience, both survey research for another purpose, and engaging with and interviewing academics, this seems a quite reasonable and plausible supposition.

councils (responsible for REF) and the research councils, came under the single umbrella of UKRI, a joint statement was issued on impact, reflecting a shared understanding across the various research councils and bodies, while each could take a nuanced view, appropriate to its scope, separately. That statement, later absorbed by UKRI and referenced by it, was issued by HEFCE, RCUK and Universities UK. In itself, the *Joint Statement* was reflective and open. It incorporated a long chain of possibilities, among which, 'a contribution to cultural life' could be found. Other aspects identified started with industry and business (reflecting, perhaps, the priority concerns of the funding bodies), also including healthcare and social well-being, public policy, contributions to public debate and 'improved understanding of the world we live in.'[18] The statement recognised that impact could stem from individual pieces of research, or from bodies of research over a long time (whether by individuals, or teams), and could be collaborative across departments both within and across different research organisations. The key, in this statement, was recognition of the 'broad and diverse' range of impacts and means of making a difference and bringing benefit.

The new UKRI incorporated this *Joint Statement*, with its fresh and strong branding putting 'knowledge with impact' to the forefront.[19] However, the initial UKRI website definition (while it envisaged review of impact definitions and approaches), could be seen to be retrograde in relation to the approach, even though the latter was embraced and referenced, at the same time. In the most generic terms, UKRI cast impact as 'the demonstrable contribution that excellent research makes to society and the economy.'[20] This was supplemented with recognition that impact could occur in 'many ways' including 'creating and sharing new knowledge and innovation, inventing groundbreaking new products, companies and jobs, developing new and improving existing public services and policy, enhance quality of life and health, and many more.' Economic and societal impact was also clearly segregated from academic impact, with the impact definition gaining the clarification that the contribution could be

---

18 HEFCE, RCUK and Universities UK, *Joint Statement on Impact* available at www. ukri.org/files/legacy/innovation/jointstatementimpact-pdf/

19 Motty Long, 'UKRI's rebrand promotes "knowledge with impact"', *Design Week*, 22 October 2019.

20 UKRI, 'Excellence With Impact' available at www.ukri.org/innovation/excellence-eith-impact (accessed at 13 November 2019).

'of benefit to individuals, organisations and nations.' As such, while relatively generic and open, this joint approach could be seen not to be especially inviting, for example, to the arts and cultural sectors, and those researching in them. Of course, 'and many more' would allow for contributions in these fields, as could the mission to 'enhance the quality of life.' But, given past problems of interpretation, the exclusion of specific references, while heavily emphasising economy and society, with strong references to business, policy and health could give the impression (as many subject areas, perhaps including Politics and International Studies, interpreted it) that certain areas were more prized.

Despite the possible narrowness (while, ironically, being broad and open) of the UKRI definition, notwithstanding that it also incorporated the *Joint Statement* by its predecessors, the sense of what impact meant settled down, after a decade of novelty and exploration. Also under the broad umbrella of UKRI, REF2021 confirmed the embedded understanding that was emerging by opting to keep the same definition used in REF2014. However, this was supplemented with useful strands of suggestion for how 'effects on, change and benefit to' might be taken — but, to which impact was 'not limited.'[21] These were:

•   the activity, attitude, awareness, behaviour, capacity, opportunity, performance, policy, practice, process, or understanding
•   of an audience, beneficiary, community, constituency, organisation or individuals
•   in any geographic, location whether locally, regionally, nationally or internationally

This guidance also made clear that 'reduction or prevention or harm, risk, cost or other negative effects' were embraced by the REF interpretation and understanding of impact. Broadly, this offered generous scope to explore and understand impact in as rounded and open a manner as possible — but, all boiling down to the simple sense in which we have approached the term and the phenomenon throughout this volume: academic research (of an assumed quality) that makes a difference of some kind in the world. However, despite the relative

---

21 REF, *Guidance on Submissions* REF 2019/01, Bristol: REF (Department for the Economy NI, HEFCW, Research England and Scottish Funding Council), January 2019, p. 68.

clarity and breadth in these understandings, impact remained obscure, intimidating and regarded, in the institutional sense, as too narrow by many. We take this up in the following section.

Understanding impact: problems and issues

Despite the relative openness and breadth, as well as the straightforward and inviting simplicity of key official approaches to impact, many in the academic world have not seen it this way. Some regard the approach as too narrow; others see it as ambiguous; and there are those who simply reject the impact agenda as another, unnecessary, anti-academic, bureaucratic demand.[22] In the present section, we will explore some of these problems and issues, alongside discussion of areas that possibly make some academics feel daunted by the question of impact — namely around how it is identified. It is perhaps this practical aspect of the topic, associated with identifying it, that generates unease and rejection, and makes grasping that which impact means harder, we assess, than it is.

The first issue to confront is (some) researchers' scepticism and outright antagonism to the term impact. Despite openness and attempts to be as inclusive as possible in the framing of impact, significant portions of the British academic community questioned and challenged the introduction of a more official and institutional approach to impact, as REF2014 included impact in the evaluation framework. For some, this was a matter of bearing additional burdens. So many of the researchers with whom we have engaged at King's and elsewhere initially only thought of impact as another thing to do — and it was one that they were so often reluctant to do and rejected. Impact was seen as nothing more than a great, additional burden, both on individuals and institutions, as they had to struggle to come to terms with it and prepare submissions.[23] There could be no doubt that most researchers in the ever more pressurised and bureaucratised UK university sector would recognise something in this sense of weights to be carried, all impinging on and, possibly, corrupting their core research mission, simply by constraining the time and space for research — and,

22 See John O'Regan and John Gray, 'The Bureaucratic Distortion of Academic Work', *Language and Intercultural Communication* Vol. 18, No. 5, 2018, pp. 533–48.

23 Simon Smith, Vicky Ward and Allan House, '"Impact" in the Proposals for the UK's Research Excellence Framework: Shifting the Boundaries of Academic Autonomy', *Research Policy* Vol. 40, No. 1, 2011.

no doubt, those in Australia, the Netherlands and elsewhere responding to similar trends would find all of this familiar, too. Yet, to a considerable extent, the weight to be borne was, at least partially, misjudged.

Seeing impact as an additional burden clearly missed the core point that making a difference could be part of that which academics, in any subject, were 'doing' anyway with their research. Indeed, for most academics we interacted with this was the case, as it was the very reason we engaged with them. So, many researchers needed only gently to understand that impact was something they were 'doing' anyway. It was not necessarily an additional burden — although should they become involved in writing case studies for REF submission, it could be.[24] For others, as signalled in the introduction to this chapter, it was believed to be anathema. The supposedly new element of 'impact' was an intrusion into, and a corruption of, the pure and pristine world of academic autonomy.[25] This was the ivory tower university world where self-governance and the virtues of peer evaluation were necessary and sufficient, following Smith *et al.* — which also had concerns that attention to impact could distort research scope, or type. Going beyond, echoing Bourdieu, this was a world in which the smaller and narrower the group of scholars involved, the greater the autonomy and the purer, more refined and more authentic, and certainly more autonomous, the quest for knowledge and understanding.[26] Concern for impact and the real world, for some, was an impingement on academic freedom and autonomy.[27] It was a 'Frankenstein's monster', in the catchy title of Martin's account.[28]

---

24 Whilst hard to disentangle from the wider effects of REF, evidence of increased activity included both the emergence of leadership roles and research positions, as both authors experienced. This is also true of the added financial expenditure linked to the REF exercise.

25 Others have also suggested that there is the potential that REF impact simply reinforces current hierarchies of power within the discipline. Katherine Smith and Ellen Stewart, 'We Need to Talk about Impact: Why Social Policy Academics Need to Engage with the UK's Research Impact Agenda', *Journal of Social Policy* Vol. 46, No. 1, 2017, pp. 109–27; Emily Yarrow and Julie Davies, 'The Gendered Impact Agenda', *LSE Impact Blog*, 8 March 2018.

26 Pierre Bourdieu, 'The Specificity of the Scientific Field and the Social Conditions of the Progress of Reason', *Information — International Social Science Council* Vol. 14, No. 6, 1975.

27 R. Watermeyer, 'Lost in the "third space": the impact of public engagement in higher education on academic identity, research practice and career progression', *European Journal of Higher Education* Vol. 5, No. 3, 2015.

28 B.R. Martin, 'The Research Excellence Framework and the "impact agenda": Are we creating a Frankenstein's monster?' *Research Evaluation* Vol. 20, No. 3, 2011.

There was surely an ever-present cause to be concerned about and to seek to preserve the development of knowledge from infections and distortions. Yet, this was a notional sense of academic freedom and the integrity of a self-governing academic world that had long passed. In the image at the end of F. Scott Fitzgerald's *The Great Gatsby*, these were academics beating on, boats against the current, borne back ceaselessly into a past that receded before them.[29]

In reality, academic tenure, the touchstone and immune system of academic freedom and autonomy, had long been ceded in the UK, removed by Prime Minister Margaret Thatcher's governments during the 1980s, at the birth of the trend to make every part of society and the public sector accountable, including — and notably — universities. While tenure remained a prized asset in the US, where most of the famous universities were private institutions and so (relatively) free from calls for public accountability, growing pressures from government, both via funding and other moves, meant that tenure and academic freedom were ever more constrained. The projection of autonomy, however desirable and, ultimately, however valuable (even in an arguably compromised form), failed to reflect the realities of the 21st century. It is hard, however much there is sympathy for the ideal of pure academic enterprise, not to recognise the realities of funding, including the need for it and the likely prospect that most funders will enjoy the idea that their funding might help to make a difference.[30] It is equally hard not to agree with Derrick that a 'more balanced approach' is needed, that clinging to chimeric ideas of pure academic autonomy is 'destructive' and that it would be better to focus on 'how to make the system work better.'[31] Moreover, as she also points out, there is a social contract involved between researchers and publics, and in this 'two-way' relationship researchers benefiting from public funds

29 Clearly, far more research is needed before it is possible to determine the full effect of the impact agenda on research.
30 The Leverhulme Trust is a stand-out exception, here, especially after the shift towards consideration of impact at the Harry Frank Guggenheim Foundation. The Leverhulme Trust, while not averse to any wider impacts that might arise from research it funds — there is no objection to impact, *per se* — has no expectation of impact. Indeed, in some cases, it is willing to commit the research funding to back individuals — another exceptional and unusual position — and be content that the researchers simply get on and carry out research, purely for its own sake, without any further demands.
31 Gemma Derrick, *The Evaluator's Eye: Impact Assessment and Academic Peer Review*, Cham: Palgrave Macmillan, 2018, p. 35.

have a 'duty', some of the time, at least, to help 'make the world a better place.'[32]

Beyond rejections of impact arising from worldviews, and at times partial misunderstandings, the sense of fuzziness around impact was a concern in the academic community, even among those seriously engaging with it as members of REF panels. Perceptions veered, and would continue to do so, from the sense that impact was open, vague and 'nebulous', to innate feelings that it was too narrowly cast, recognising only particular kinds of impact,[33] thus distorting real consideration of it. These patterns are well attested in Derrick's excellent research with REF panel members, where some had ideas of applied research and only that was impact, so the wide scope of the definition given was too broad, while others found the definition too narrow, as with many scholars not formally involved in evaluation, and judged that it was limiting and their own sense of impact was broader.[34] As Derrick also found, much of the time, preconceptions and personal perspectives on impact changed for most evaluators during the process. This gave the impression that, through their exchanges, social experience and common understanding, most (though certainly not all) had come to regard the REF scope for impact as right, in its openness, its scope and its inclusiveness, both of research and of impact.

The point that most of these evaluators reached is something that, in the end, indicates that official definition of impact was neither too narrow and pressured, nor too broad. To the extent that there was ambiguity, or openness, this was a positive feature, as it allowed for many species of impact to be presented to the evaluators, and gave the sense that research and impact across a range of areas was both more varied and extensive than might have been presumed. Quite plausibly, the problems, where they existed, about the scope of impact were not embedded in the official definition, or approach, but in the prior biases of the evaluators, to a large extent.[35] On this basis, it is reasonable to consider, not only that impact became a part of the academic agenda that would only grow in importance, but also that, for the most part, perceptions of the official definition of impact as either too narrow or

---

32 Derrick, *The Evaluator's Eye*, p. 29.
33 Derrick, *The Evaluator's Eye*, p. 101.
34 Derrick, *The Evaluator's Eye*, pp. 69–72, 101–4, 111–14.
35 This certainly reflected some of our encounters with those making decisions on REF2014 submissions.

too broad, were misplaced. That definition allowed the thousand flowers of impact to bloom — or, more precisely, the 3,709 pathways to impact identified by Jonathan Grant and his team.[36] Yet, to be sure, there remained two areas where some involved wondered if the definition of impact should clearly include news media and processes of engagement, particularly, public engagement. This was something that would be in line with the feelings, perceptions and expectations of most researchers, anyway (and these were, it seems, incorporated by REF panels, despite the definition and guidance, albeit as a softer, or weaker, aspect of impact[37]). Processes of engagement are treated in the next chapter, preceded by discussion of the issue of news media 'impact.'

36 King's College London and Digital Science, *The nature, scale and beneficiaries of research impact: An initial analysis of Research Excellence Framework (REF) 2014 impact case studies*, Research Report 2015/01, Prepared for the Higher Education Funding Council of England, Higher Education Funding Council for Wales, Scottish Funding Council, Department of Employment and Learning Northern Ireland, Research Councils UK and the Wellcome Trust, London: HEFCE, 2015.

37 See Derrick, *The Evaluator's Eye*, pp. 102–3 and 117–20. The way evaluators appear to have embraced public engagement and news media 'impact', despite guidance, features in our examination of world-leading impact in Chapter 4.

3 Impact — towards a typology

Having given definition to 'impact' as a concept and introduced understanding of some of the problems and issues associated with it, in Chapter 2, we now turn to developing the concept by considering what it is not — that is, we discuss news media and public engagement because they present problems: most researchers understand them to be important aspects of impact, while research funders and others with institutional perspectives, reject them. This is an issue which relates, in part, to the quadripartite typology of impact we set out later in the chapter. That typology relates to more established notions of instrumental, conceptual and capacity-building modes of making a difference, and adds a potential, possibly weaker and more controversial, fourth type, procedural (or phenomenological) impact — which might also be related to media and public engagement notions. This filters through Chapters 6 and 7, and is revisited in the final chapter. All this is preceded by discussion of issues surrounding the 'official' impact agenda, including that which it is not supposed to include and questions of presenting it.

What impact is not (?): news media 'impact' and public engagement

Almost universally, when first talking to anyone about 'impact', the first understanding of it involved gaining some kind of news media attention — to be quoted or interviewed in the printed news, or interviewed on broadcast news, was to have impact.[1] This was true when

---

1 Almost every researcher whom we engaged, at any stage of our interest in impact, has started with the understanding that impact was about contributions to, or reporting of research in, news media outlets.

the impact agenda first emerged, towards the end of the first decade of the 21st century, and it remained just as true a decade later. As should be clear from the discussion above, this understanding was not in line with emerging 'official' versions of the concept. Indeed, for the proclaimed purposes of those setting the exam questions for research impact, officially, it is no impact, or no evidence of impact, at all.[2] However, for its own sake, it is worth discussing both contributions to news media and presentations of evidence to potential users in the context of impact study — and reality. It is worth reflecting on how far media coverage constitutes 'impact', not only because it represents more commonplace understanding and is important for the path to consideration of impact *qua* impact, as understood and used by official bodies, but also because, whatever the official designations, there might be more to this than officially allowed, as will be seen in Chapters 7 and 8, later.

The media connection is, perhaps, an obvious step from dissemination. As mentioned briefly in the Introduction, early interest in impact concerned the challenge of how to get beyond simple research presentation. There was — and, no doubt, will remain for a long time — an issue around briefing ministers, or government officials, for example, or presenting evidence to a Parliamentary, or Congressional, committee, or to a public inquiry. While potentially significant, whether simply as recognition for the individual, or group, involved in sharing their knowledge and understanding, or, more notably, for any attention taken of it, there was little reason necessarily to assume that any attention of real note was taken. In general, this activity could be summarised as 'input' — as distinct from 'impact.'

However, the line separating input and impact is not completely clear, much of the time. As noted in some of the pioneering discussion of what would later become labelled impact (already mentioned in the Introduction),[3] the problem was the route from dissemination to difference, one that could be difficult to trace (as discussed in the following section on process). It could justifiably be judged that any researchers invited to present evidence to a Parliamentary committee, or to brief a government minister, had already been noticed by those who made the invitation — so, in some sense, the researchers had

---

2 This is an issue that we shall revisit in the Conclusion, in light of the analysis that we present in Chapter 7.
3 Sandra M. Nutley, Isabel Walter and Huw Davies, *Using Evidence: How Research Can Inform Public Services*, Bristol: Policy Press, 2007.

made some degree of impact. If the request to give evidence arose from particular pieces of research (instead of general recognition of research standing, for now), then it would seem reasonable to suppose that the research had already achieved a minimal degree of 'influence.' At least, the research had prompted someone to want to find out more about the findings, and to benefit from the assessment of whomever had conducted the research, and so forth. In terms that were used in the protean phases of impact study, it might be judged that this research, whatever it was, had been 'applied', if only in the limited sense that the event at which research was presented was something that could not have happened otherwise.

It is hard fully to gauge this hypothetical instance without a real-world, empirical example, as the devil would be in the detail of judging the extent to which this 'impact' had any real significance. Without further information, this would most likely be a 'shallow' impact. It relies, to some degree, on interpretation of 'application', as a notion, and, perhaps, influence could be said to be used in a limited way. Often, we could suppose, influence in this form might result in little of true note, because processes such as legislative scrutiny generally involve evidence gathering from invited individuals. So, those invited might simply be there to fill slots in a process (albeit, chosen ahead of others). But, conversely, sometimes, of course, the result might be something of considerable distinction. It can be hard to be sure, perhaps, whether the invitation and the evidence add up to acknowledgement that research has been beneficial and of value. In the end, the degree to which these contributions count might only, really, be confirmed by other corroborating evidence — for example, references (particularly if they are significant and meaningful ones) in committee reports. This will determine the salience of any effect to be derived from this kind of engagement. This form of engagement, more often than not, it might be supposed, makes weaker, rather than stronger, impact more probable and more frequent. Yet, as noted above, all of this probably constitutes impact of some kind, even if perhaps soft, and it is certainly something that researchers feel and see as impact.

To return to the issue of news and similar coverage with which we began this section, applying a similar logic, it could be possible to see 'use' by journalists, or publishers, which would, in a narrow sense, give them benefit from research. This is because the research would have assisted their fulfilling their business, as communication tools and, also, as commercial or public bodies. In this sense, the press coverage might be seen as an example of impact; none the less, it would be a relatively weak one. As with dissemination and other forms of engagement, already discussed, viewing this as impact, while not thoroughly out of the question, by any measure, depends on narrow reading and interpretation. In this instance, the relevant interpretation would relate to 'use' and 'benefit'. Such usage could, in principle, also apply to the presentation of any given information. That would mean our viewing the comings and goings of celebrities, as covered by newspapers and websites, as 'use' by news media for their 'benefit.' And, this perspective would not be unreasonable, as the news organisations certainly 'use' the information to fill space and to combine attracting audiences and making money. That benefits those on the business side, but, also, it should be recognised, the publics consuming the output of news organisations. Just as in the case of presenting to officials, or offering testimony to legislative committees, there is no guarantee, however, of the quality and depth involved. This is because impact, and tracing it, might be quite a challenge. This is a topic considered in the final sections of this chapter, as we consider the ways in which the idea of impact might be conceived and applied beyond its mere definition and, then, outline the elements of a typology of impact.

Process, research engagement and beyond

It is important to recognise that impact has different dimensions, as tracing effects is widely acknowledged to be a problematic business.[4] It would be impossible to discuss all of these aspects here and the problems of tracing them — with over 3,000 impact pathways identified among the Research Excellence Framework (REF)2014 impact case studies, a book ten times the length of this one might not be able to capture all of them fully. Moreover, what might be assumed to be the *sui generis*, species-specific character of those individual elements simply could not be put into operation in a study of this kind; and nor would they be terribly useful for readers, unless, by chance, they recognised exactly the same feature in their own world. Better to understand the capturing of impact and, so, the concept and nature of impact itself, it is more helpful to consider the ways, or arenas, in which impact might be identified. It is useful, in this context, to identify the middle ground between the definition of impact and its myriad particular manifestations. That middle ground includes enhanced understanding

---

4 Nutley *et al.*, *Using Evidence*.

of how impact can be identified and elaboration of a framework to distinguish between different types of impact, all of which make a difference of some kind.

A key problem with the reception and understanding of impact among academics has been the relative simplicity and naïvety with which it has been welcomed. In part, those presenting the requirement played a role in this, especially in the way REF2014 appeared, and was certainly understood, to seek a direct and explicit connection from research to impact: here is a piece of internationally excellent research, here is how and where it was published and communicated, here is the difference it made. This is a direct and linear interpretation of how research might lead to impact. In applied research, certainly, this could generally be expected to be the case: a research question is posed for practical need, the research is undertaken, it produces relevant findings, those findings are adopted and applied by the relevant user. But, both those who only thought of applied research as research with impact and also those who thought that applied research was not properly research discovered the narrowness and weakness of their approaches in REF2014. Furthermore, as one of the interviewees in Derrick's outstanding research noted, the intended impact of applied research might not be its only one, or even its most extensive, citing the example of Teflon, specifically developed in the US for coating NASA's spaceships, but widely exploited in pots and pans for cooking (and, we might add, clothing and many other uses).[5]

In reality, while many of the models used as the institutional impact agenda developed had a linear character, including progression and feedback loops, making a difference comes in many and varied forms. There is certainly a variable geometry, with impact often occurring through direct engagement long before publications relating to it are in print. Moreover, the patterns of research, communication, sharing and use are often extensive and diverse. One challenge, often, is to link one piece of research, among many others, to a designated difference. One reason why the breadth and openness of the institutional definition of impact was actually so important is that it permitted the presentation, exploration and evaluation of multiple and diverse contributions. Those contributions did not need to be of equal volume. The key issue was whether the research contribution was necessary to the outcome.

5 Gemma Derrick, *The Evaluator's Eye: Impact Assessment and Academic Peer Review*, Cham: Palgrave Macmillan, 2018, p. 101.

If research could be seen to be an essential part of a research and impact story, then, no matter its 'size', it was a necessary component and its share in the claimed impact was justified and equal. The research contribution did not have to be equal in amount done, nor did any piece of research need to be sufficient to the impact claimed. But, it did need to show that it was necessary.

The key concept for understanding this process is 'centricity', as Derrick shows. Describing how panels in REF2014 approached this matter, developing a centricity strategy, she shows how the concept helped to manage complexity and to identify the value of contributions:

> ... if a smaller claim of Impact was considered by the panel as an essential pre-cursor (attributable) to another larger downstream Impact, then both Impacts were considered essential and valued equally.[6]

This recognised that most impact was far from simple to present and certainly not linear. It was a matter of judging if a particular claim made could, with fair reason, be associated with eventual impact described. As one of Derrick's interlocutors is quoted, 'was the research essential for that Impact?' If research involved two universities, but only one chose to submit a case study, even if the one deciding not to submit was responsible for substantively more significant parts of the research, the submitting university was entirely justified, so long as its own contribution could be seen to be necessary and intrinsic to the case study. That was enough for the contribution to impact to be established: '... if that research was vital in order for that Impact to occur, then we would usually accept it even if other institutions had also contributed to it.'[7] This sensibly reflected the reality that, even in the most straightforward and apparently linear of cases, the research-impact relationship is better understood as a whole ecology, rather than as a chain. It involves a multitude of interlocking and mutually dependent components, both of research and impact, meaning that rarely can one piece of research equal one example of impact. Or, using another analogy that was used in REF2014: if there is an inverse tree, with impact at the fanned-out top, and if a claim was on that tree somewhere, then it was valued equally with all other parts of the tree. This was an 'on-off' evaluation — did it make a contribution, or not?

6 Derrick, *The Evaluator's Eye*, p. 122.
7 Derrick, *The Evaluator's Eye*, p. 123.

If it did, then it shared in the overall assessment of the impact case study.[8] Thus, any contribution to research and impact is part of a complex ecology, or part of a cloud, in which it has a necessary place.[9] It is a part of a process.

Tracing how research has been translated into application, as we have seen, can often be a challenging affair, with pathways hard to navigate with certainty and evidence often opaque. Hence, the value of conceiving of the research-impact link as an ecosystem, a cloud, or an inverse tree, and a process. This was a major consideration for those who initially embarked on trying to identify when research became beneficially applied, or, how dissemination became difference, in practice. In this context, processes were both vital aspects of analysis, but, also, it was argued, with very good reason, could be manifestations of impact, themselves.[10]

Process could, then, be a first element in developing a framework for categorising forms of impact. Early evidence on research use indicated that process impact, as a type, was the most identifiable way in which impact occurred and should not be overlooked.[11] However, it was not necessarily easier to confirm much of the time than were other types of impact. Indeed, they may sometimes have been harder to gauge, given that the process itself might not have offered clear points for evaluation. This tallies with observations and

---

8 At least one of Derrick's informants had a concern about 'piggybacking' in one instance, but concluded that it was 'fine', in the context, which was hard to evaluate. Derrick, *The Evaluator's Eye*, pp. 124–5.

9 Of course, as a caveat, we should be aware that because the issue was seen this way in the past is no guarantee that it would always be regarded that way. Clearly, it created some discomfort and it might be that a quantitatively more substantial contribution, rather than simply a necessary one, could emerge. However, both the logic of necessity — it is, or it is not — and the general desire and commitment of those managing institutional impact questions to maintain consistency suggest that, for official purposes, at least, the size of contribution would remain less important than the essence of it.

10 It is important in this context to be conceptually clear about the distinction between process as type of impact and processes that lead to other forms of impact. The point here is to note process as a type of impact. As stated earlier, processes can have impact in and of themselves. But, they do not necessarily do so. Processes can lead to other types of impact, without the process itself necessarily registering as a type of impact. Thus, it is vital to maintain a clear distinction between instances where it is the process itself that generates impact and examples where process leads to an impact of another kind (and noting that on some occasions both might be present together, in which case, each should be discretely identified).

11 Nutley *et al.*, *Using Evidence*.

sentiments in research on REF2014, where, evidently, some evaluators had a strong sense that engagement was an element of impact, even if, in the case of public engagement, as noted above, there might not be enough sense of what difference that engagement made. However, it is clear that the research process itself, irrespective of other outcomes and findings, can make a difference — as happened with one of our own research projects (which also made notable, tangible differences).[12]

The notion of process is an important element in understanding impact — and how it is produced, identified and can be shown. In reality, simply engaging with research users makes a difference of some kind, sometimes (even if that difference can be hard to detail empirically, or to trace how it operated). This is a view shared by others who have considered impact in the context of international studies — indeed, who stress this as the key way in which to understand impact in political frames: impact is 'more about the conversation pursued than the consequences achieved' and any version that 'measures the outcome rather than the process sets academics up to fail.'[13] We do not accept this proposition entirely — our research shows outcomes that make a difference and can be gauged; but, we concur that it is a significant aspect of impact, albeit not officially embraced. It is a notion of impact confirmed by 'users', who acknowledged that the process of interaction itself had made a difference, of some kind, giving perhaps a greater sense of value than often attributed to the term 'effect on' in the REF definition of impact — one 'user' stated that the 'process of engagement ... helped the MoD [Ministry of Defence] broaden its thinking and inform its internal policy debate.'[14] It was clearly hard to specify in detail what happened with thinking and how the debate was informed; but, there was no doubt that the process of research engagement had had some 'effect.'

---

12 Our research on art and reconciliation had an impact on one of our partners, for example, the History Museum of Bosnia and Hercegovina, which re-conceptualised parts of its mission to become an open and 'living museum', engaging in more, and new activities, related to those we had introduced in the course of our collaboration. Dr. Rachel Kerr, Professor James Gow, Dr. Denisa Kostovičova and Dr. Paul Lowe, 'Art and Reconciliation: Conflict Culture and Community' (AH/P005365/1).

13 Christopher R. Moran and Christopher S. Browning, 'REF impact and the discipline of politics and international studies', *British Politics* Vol. 13 2018, p. 256.

14 A senior figure in the Ministry of Defence in London strongly suggested that it was the process itself that made the difference, rather than any clearly defined change.

Towards a typology of impact: conceptual; instrumental; capacity building; procedural

One thing absent from research on REF2014 and the way in which the broad definition of impact was mapped on to micro-detail in research, which was, in turn, mapped on to an assessment of impact, is conceptualisation of the research-impact nexus. The foregoing discussion indicates that researchers have a sense that news media and public engagement constitute a category of impact, but that this was not officially recognised and endorsed, and also that, more clearly (and of more positively ambiguous status), research engagement and the research and research-engagement processes should be regarded in this way. Yet, there is no sense of what other forms impact might take — and, largely, these are only identified because they are problematic, in that researchers and evaluators have the sense that these are valid categories, but they do not easily fit with the institutional definition of impact. Clearly, however, it would be of help to evaluators and to all engaged in understanding impact (and seeking to interpret and present it), if there were analytical tools to help more easily identify whether particular points of research have had impact. In this final section of the chapter, we explore and set out a heuristic framework for answering the questions: 'is this impact?'; 'has this had impact?'

From the preceding discussion, it might be supposed that, reflecting most researchers' sense of the issues, news media and public engagement might be a type of impact, as would be research engagement, or the process of research and engagement. While the first of these, as already discussed, is, at best, a very weak form of impact and perhaps better not considered under the research impact rubric itself, process is a clearly recognised element in early research relating to impact, as also noted already, albeit that research was identifying steps towards and degrees of impact, rather than categorising different types of impact. However, not even process impact is considered in the one typology that was attempted, which we have been able to identify, and certainly not news media impact. This was a seemingly little noticed and even less used typology developed under the auspices of the Economic and Social Research Council (ESRC) in the very early days of institutional impact discussions. Though far from beyond question, as will be seen, this was a useful and robust attempt to make it easier to understand what impact could mean and it is quite surprising that its trident of instrumental, conceptual and capacity-building forms of impact has not been more widely picked up and discussed, and even put to work in the world of impact research, understanding and evaluation.

The categories identified in the ESRC's treatment of impact offer a helpful trio of impact types:[15]

• Conceptual
• Instrumental
• Capacity building

The first of these concerns all examples of impact — because every instance of impact, in some way, involves some change in thinking. Conceptual may include contributing to the understanding of an issue or related issues. This might mean identifying new ways of conceptualising a phenomenon, or reframing debates. However, it might equally mean providing challenges and a process whereby previous, or existing thinking is enhanced and reinforced — while most of the most obvious impact might clearly point to change, in moments such as this one, the notion of effect is important, because there has been an effect, which is to keep understanding as it was. Of course, even in this example, there has been some change, viz. the process of challenge and the testing of existing understanding. The key is that there has been an effect on how something is conceived.

Instrumental impact addresses the areas in which most researchers might most obviously envisage making a difference. For example, this could include influencing the development of policy, practice or service provision (including the development of medicines and therapies, as well as enhancing business or social provision), shaping legislation, and altering behaviour (whether in individuals, groups, organisations, or whole societies and polities, and internationally). Beyond these types of action, which are the ones that most commonly occur in official considerations, it might also cover the ways in which research could contribute to, and have an effect on, visual practice and arts exhibitions, the role of the arts in social contexts, or theatrical productions (whether dramatic, or musical). In each instance, the central element is that use has been made of the research in a way that has benefited those making that use.

The third category in this typology is capacity building. This form of impact clearly entails elements of each of the other two. What distinguishes it is the focus on growth. While a growth in the wherewithal to do something might well apply to non-human resources, such as

---

15 *Taking Stock: A Summary of ESRC's Work to Evaluate the Impact of Research on Policy and Practice*, ESRC, February 2009.

energy, it is most often thought of and used with regard to human beings, whether as individuals, or in larger groups of whatever kind. This might entail, for example, the way in which research can enhance technical, or personal skill development. This might mean stronger knowledge and understanding of a place, or a field that enables a larger number, or a wider group, of individuals to do something. The key to this type of impact is that doing something has been enhanced, improved or expanded.

However, while useful, this tripartite typology contains two problems. One, not so serious for a good idea, is that the last of these — capacity building — does not actually appear in the literature cited for it. This is not such a great issue, as clearly, the content of the point, if not its attribution, is sound: capacity building, notably through skill development, can be judged to be a good example and indication of impact. The second problem with the trilogy is that other potential forms of impact that can be identified in parts of the literature, and have been already in this section, are excluded, including the notion that impact can stem from the processes of research engagement and research, and research engagement — where process has some 'effect' but no tangible outcome is defined. Should these other terms be added to a typology of impact?

There is a logical robustness to the three forms of impact identified — they clearly involve outcomes that are distinct, albeit that instrumental and capacity building inevitably embrace the conceptual, as well. As will be recalled, one of the problems with the idea of news media and public engagement impact is the serious limitation that they involve no evident outcome, beyond the fact of their having occurred. Beyond this, they rest on assumptions that something could, or even must, have occurred because of them. This provides a test for other possible types of impact that could be included in the framework. Two such candidates emerge from critical reflection on the question of impact in both older and more recent literature, as discussed above, and particularly from the sensibilities revealed in Derrick's landmark study of impact evaluation and evaluators: impact may be detected as a phenomenon and a process.

Phenomenological impact involves the generation of attention, such as reporting on research findings, as part of a process. It includes the phenomenon of gaining attention, which, on the basis of the research conducted for this study, is how most researchers initially conceive of impact — a form of celebration and celebrity. However, the generation of attention, while clearly a form of impact, in line with a meteor strike on the crust of the earth, has no sense of making a difference, beyond the fact of its existence. While phenomenological impact in this sense is one welcomed and used by politicians, marketing executives and celebrities alike (when positive, although the last of these categories might well also welcome at least some negative attention) — it is, at best, a weak form of impact, in the final analysis. There could be no necessary assumption that the attention the research received, in whatever forum, would lead to societal effects. In this sense, it is aligned with and perhaps a broader category of news media impact, as discussed above. These types of 'weak' impact fall well short of 'true' impact on the most demanding scales, such as the seven-level reception-impact ladder developed by Knott and Wildavsky and discussed above.

None the less, consideration of this type of impact should not wholly be excluded from discussion and evaluation of impact, in general. It is valuable to note that such impact can occur, irrespective of other levels or types of impact. Impact as a phenomenon corresponds to the standard at which most researchers, heretofore, at least, appear to have considered impact beyond the scholarly idiom at all. It is arguable, on this basis, that it should be included in a typology of impact. However, while clearly recognised and perceived to be impact by researchers and users, as not only existing research, but also as our research presented in Chapter 7 indicates, in the end, the absence of a clear outcome suggests that it might be better regarded as only supplemental to other forms of impact and so to include it in a conceptual typology could be misleading and fail the intended heuristic purpose.

If phenomenological impact is to be excluded, while being acknowledged as a weak form of impact, this leaves the question of procedural impact. Should the clear sense identified in the literature that process is an important aspect of impact give it a place in the typology? Procedural impact involves direct interaction with users, who might not necessarily adopt research findings, or transform their activity in relation to it, but whose engagement and interest are evident, perhaps, for example, in continuing interactions. It is also notable that Nutley and her colleagues found process impact to be the most extensive and commonly identified, as noted earlier. Moreover, the potential impact simply of the research or engagement processes themselves is recognised in other major studies.[16] In their 'ladder' of research use, Landry *et al.* use the term 'cognition' for the second

---

16 Nutley *et al.*, *Using Evidence*; R. Landry, N. Amara and M. Lamari, 'Climbing the Ladder of Research Utilization', *Science Communication* Vol. 22 No. 4 2001.

rung — the first one, reading across, above the level of that which is clearly 'input'. At this level, which can overlap with, but is not precisely the same as procedural impact, policy makers and practitioners have recognised and 'understood' research, but there has been no definitive further impact.[17] In some cases, it is perhaps central to the methodology for evaluating impact.[18] This gives credibility to its inclusion in a typology of impacts. Even more, perhaps, so does the inclusion of the term in the REF2021, albeit as an example of an impact-relevant activity that constituted a subject still in need of an object and a location, as presented.

However, procedural impact sits at a boundary and could be seen as close to conceptual impact, depending on how narrowly, or broadly, the latter is drawn. As noted above, some view process as an important category because, while it might be thought, for example, to broaden thinking, it does not reach the level that might robustly be considered to be 'conceptual.' While, in some sense, 'broadening thinking' might be stretched to meet the notion of 'conceptual' impact, it is probably better judged to be a distinct phenomenon and better regarded as such, if there is to be a fuller understanding of impact. If 'conceptual' must have a clear outcome — a new way of thinking, classifying or describing, then 'procedural' impact remains at a level where it is felt, or judged, by those involved to have been useful, but it is not possible to characterise, or clearly delineate, or define, the impact itself. Of course, if that sense of having been affected in a somewhat diffuse way is regarded as 'conceptual', then the case for process impact is less strong. Yet, clearly, there has been an impact that the 'user' believes had value, even if that value remains amorphous and without conceptualisation. Given the sense of value, in instances such as this, such impact should not be discarded. However, it cannot properly be regarded as conceptual, given that it lacks any rigour and clarity.

Even in instances where the process also leads to other impacts, procedural impact remains a distinct phenomenon that should be identified, just as conceptual and instrumental should both be identified where both occur. However, some form of procedural impact might, often, be the most likely to occur. Certainly, it is a form of

17 Landry *et al.*, 'Climbing the Ladder'.
18 Steven Wooding, Edward Nason, Lisa Klautzer, Jennifer Rubin, Stephen Hanney and Jonathan Grant, *Policy and practice impacts of research funded by the Economic and Social Research Council: A case study of the Future of Work programme, approach and analysis*, Cambridge: Rand Europe, 2007.

impact that policy and practice users, as well as researchers, acknowledge and recognise — even where research impact on policy and policy debates might, at best, be mixed and generally quite limited, as could be expected to be the case, more often than not. Process, or procedural impact might be vague in some senses and lack a precise sense of change, but, it clearly has some form of effect, for example, evident in not infrequent comments by practitioners that research has been useful as general background to discussion. It is beneficial, then, to add procedural impact to the three ESRC terms and include it in a typology, albeit with the proviso that, if the reading of 'conceptual' is broad and loose, then the sense of recognition that something beneficial has happened without being able to specify it in instrumental or capacity building, or more stringently shaped conceptual terms, then the notion of conceptual impact might encompass it. In our view, because of the potential for uncertainty over whether an impact was conceptual enough, or not, it is a sounder approach to consider process as a distinct form of impact that involves direct interaction with users, who might not necessarily adopt research findings, or transform their activity in relation to it, but whose engagement and interest are evident in continuing interactions and who offer evidence that the process has had a beneficial effect.

By combining these elements, it is possible to arrive at a quadripartite typology that can be used practically to evaluate data on impact and which is used below:

- Instrumental
- Conceptual
- Capacity building
- Procedural

This typology permits incorporation of information that goes beyond the narrowest terms of policy and practice. It allows for inclusion of a range of impacts that have relevance and salience. It does so in an open manner that can serve the impact requirements in any discipline, or field of activity, but notably, can embrace the range of differences made in international affairs, not only in the policy world, but also in the opera house, the museum and creative industries, as well as in arts worlds, legal forums, local communities, and beyond.

When asked for examples of 'impact,' most researchers commonly turn to dissemination and input to, or engagement with, research users as evidence of impact. In some cases, this can, with reflection and further interpretation, be translated into some further form of impact.

But, this is the level at which most impact is understood and, probably, occurs. There is a disconnect here between the understanding of research impact seemingly held by a majority of researchers, irrespective of the field of research involved, and the definitions and interpretations of impact that are of interest to the research funders. There might be a case for considering this 'weak' form in impact evaluation, both in response to the general sense of that which is understood as 'impact' and a desire among funders and others to identify impact and argue that funded activity 'counts' or 'makes a difference', at all. Equally, it is likely that, over time, the more significant levels of impact generally in the sights of funding councils will come to be understood by researchers, but only through a longer-term process of discussion and socialisation. From the experience of undertaking the present study, this is likely to be a lengthy process, involving personal activity, as individuals come to grasp where and how their research has the kind of impact of interest to funding councils. For now, the standards identified above provide a typology — instrumental, conceptual, capacity building and procedural — that goes some way beyond the understanding of most investigators, but which can serve usefully as an heuristic framework. Having considered definition, problems and issues surrounding the 'official' agenda, and outlined a framework for understanding impact, we now turn to the issues of identifying and presenting world-leading research in the remaining chapters, with our own close analysis of case studies in Chapters 6 and 7, and a critical exposition of discourse analysis research, before that, in the following chapter.

4   International affairs

Although, to a large extent, debates about international relations came to be dominated by theoretical discussions, its very origins as a formal domain of study lay in impact, as indicated in the Introduction. Even as the field developed, there remained a strong sense in many quarters that international studies should retain this original purpose. In the present chapter, we present a brief historical overview. First, the chapter considers the impact question in international perspective, particularly, though not exclusively, with reference to the United States and to the realm of funders there, who provided the resources to support research and researchers who were in the business of changing societies, practices and policies, in the US and globally. The second section analyses the 'impact' of British international and security research as the impact agenda was emerging, but before REF2014 and the advent of the official institutional impact agenda. This research identifies both significant impact being developed without the pressure of REF (Research Excellence Framework) and the UK research councils, despite difficulties in capturing and expressing that research, but also a story of uneven outcomes. As we show, a number of the major UK government-research council-funded projects produced, at times, disappointing outcomes. In the final section we consider the UK REF2014 submissions to the Politics and International Studies sub-panel. In particular, we cover those that achieved 'world-leading' scores for well over 70 per cent of their impact work, even if they fell some distance from being 100 per cent. Examination of the top-rated case studies raises some questions about the assessments made, but the main conclusion reinforces the sense of underperformance in the field.

International research impact

As a field intended to have impact, there is good evidence that historically making a difference has been important. This has been an international phenomenon, albeit, perhaps, dominated by scholars from the Global North. Above all, this has been the case in the US, which, from the Second World War, at least, dominated international studies, and, which, from the early 20th century, dominated international relations, in practice. In the remainder of this section, we consider impact globally, in particular, impact in the US context.

Historically, the US has been open to scholars making a difference. From the start, its founding fathers blended intellectual exploration with government, most evident in the Federalist Papers, authored by Alexander Hamilton, James Madison and John Jay, and the writing of Thomas Jefferson. This set a template in which rotating doors would see scholars in government, under one administration, and back in their university studies when another administration took office, bringing its own academic support system with it. This openness to scholarly influence could be seen in the litany of figures holding office, from the presidency, to secretaries of state, defence, justice and more, to roles such as national security advisor. A limited sample makes this point overwhelmingly: Woodrow Wilson triggered much of the 20th-century global order; Hans J. Morgenthau and George F. Kennan defined much in the Cold War, as did Henry Kissinger and Zbigniew Brzinski; while Condoleezza Rice and Joseph Nye (who also featured in the Cold War) were instrumental in 21st-century policies of confrontation and engagement, in a sense, reinventing Morgenthau and Kennan for a new age. Of course, scholarly impact, even in this context, was uneven.[1] The example of the great Thomas Schelling showed this. His theories of communication had informed nuclear deterrence and arms control (for which he later won the Nobel Peace Prize), but when called upon to assist in helping with 'gradual action' in the context of the Vietnam War, he was 'stumped' and could offer nothing (and, shaken, his publication rate fell for the course of the Vietnam War).[2]

The commitment to research making a difference in the US could also be seen in the crucial dimension of funding. Not only did the US government system fund enormous amounts of research through official schemes, such as those that underpinned 'area studies' in the Cold War, drawing on the triangulation of language competence,

1 Duncan Bell, 'Writing the World', *International Affairs* Vol. 85 No. 1 2009, pp. 3–22.
2 Fred Kaplan, *The Wizards of Armageddon,* New York: Simon and Schuster, 1983, quoted in Jan Willem Honig, 'Uncomfortable Visions: the Rise and Decline of the Idea of Limited War' in Ben Wilkinson and James Gow, eds., *The Art of Power: Freedman on Strategy,* New York: OUP, 2018, p. 46.

disciplinary mix and deep empirical knowledge about particular places — most obviously, Russia and the other communist countries. While this fell away after the Cold War ended, the reduction of funding was reversed after the 11 September 2001 terrorist attacks, when Washington collectively realised that there was still a need for research that generated granular knowledge and understanding about peoples, places and issues that could feed into regional and global security policy.[3] This was a global requirement — not only Russia and Eurasia, or China, or the Middle East, but all regions of the world, including Europe, South Asia, South America, South-East Asia and the Pacific.

Away from government interest, throughout the Cold War and since, the major US foundations, among the biggest funders of research and action in the world, always had a principal aim of supporting research that could make a difference. The John T. and Catherine D. MacArthur Foundation, with its International Peace and Security Programme, institutional funding and other schemes, was a leader, especially in the realm of nuclear policy, arms control and regional and country studies — although, in 2017, the Foundation took the decision to channel all its resources into Nuclear Challenges, one of its longstanding mainstays.[4] Another of its programmes offered a US$100 million grant for a single proposal that promised 'real and measurable progress in solving a critical problem of our time.'[5] The Ford Foundation, the Carnegie Endowment, the US Institute of Peace, and the Woodrow Wilson International Center for Scholars all also looked to support positive change in the world — and moved funding away, if there was no evidence of a difference being made. The same was true even of small funders, such as the Harry Frank Guggenheim Foundation.[6]

---

3 The work of Alison Howell discusses some of the negative consequences of some of this type of collaboration, particularly in terms of counter-insurgency strategy. Alison Howell, 'Forget "Militarization": Race, Disability and the "Martial Politics" of the Police and of the University', *International Feminist Journal of Politics* Vol. 20 No. 2 2018, pp. 117–36.
4 See www.macfound.org/programs/ips/strategy/ available at 16 November 2019.
5 See www.macfound.org/programs/100change/ available at 16 November 2019.
6 Traditionally, the Harry Frank Guggenheim Foundation gave small grants for work on 'violence, aggression and dominance' with a completely open call and no expectation of anything beyond scholarly work — though it did have an interest in research making a difference in the world, evidenced, inter alia, by its support for what was summarised as 'the Freedman project' at King's College London, led by Gow, which sought to appreciate the nature of Professor Sir Lawrence Freedman's combination of scholarly and policy world success, with both Freedman and the Foundation 'committed to the aspiration to use the very best research possible on

Impact has been important in other contexts. The great French political theorist Raymond Aron undoubtedly had influence, and his entire theory was based on the assumption that good theory had to be useful, and to be useful it needed to be realistic and relevant to political actors.[7] This included noting the dualism of 'national' interest and other values — and why theory based only on the former was of limited purpose and how politicians, such as France's Charles de Gaulle, who espoused only the former, were naïve, missing the salience, at the time, of communist ideology. Communist ideology was, of course, vitally important in another context where research and policy were highly entwined — the Soviet Union and other communist systems, including China. In those systems, research institutes supported — and were transmission belts for — the ruling party, something that could make it hard for researchers there to understand the independence of Western academics.

In the Australian context, around half a century later, a figure such as William Maley could make a difference in various contexts, major and minor, in a changing world, mainly focused around Afghanistan. One major impact here was advising Lakhdar Brahimi, the United Nations (UN) Secretary-General's Special Representative for Afghanistan and Iraq, with others. Another, subsequently, was his assistance to the United Nations Assistance Mission in Afghanistan. At that same time, he was also informing policy via the UK Foreign and Commonwealth Office (FCO) (impact no doubt measured by his being awarded a knighthood). And at micro levels, he was often called on to help, whether with migration issues, or protecting populations — and the Australian Independent Assessment Authority, when it ignored his evidence, found itself in trouble, on the wrong side of court proceedings.[8] Maley, in the Australian context, illustrates, along with the French and US examples, that impact was and continued to be seen as an important factor of research internationally, away from the UK context and the emergence of the formal impact agenda — the topics of the following sections.

conflict and violence to work for a real and beneficial difference in the world.' James Gow and Benedict Wilkinson, 'Preface' in Benedict Wilkinson and James Gow, eds., *The Art of Creating Power: Freedman on Strategy*, London: Hurst/New York: OUP, 2017. For the Foundation itself, see www.hfg.org accessed at 29 July 2019.

7 Raymond Aron, *Peace and War: A Theory of International Relations*, New York: Doubleday, 1966.

8 *FKZ17 vs. Minister for Immigration and Border Protection and ANOR*, Federal Circuit Court of Australia, [2019] FCCA 2521.

UK research impact before 2014

This section analyses the 'impact', or potential impact, of British international affairs research at the time the impact agenda was emerging, but before REF2014 and the advent of the official institutional impact agenda. Aside from a handful of notable exceptions, such as Lawrence Freedman's contribution to UK Prime Minister Tony Blair's 'Chicago Speech' on intervention, visible examples of a real difference being made were hardly to be found — although Freedman himself was clearly an influential figure, not only in London, but also in Washington DC, and he and two others had been appointed to the UK's first ever Strategic Defence Review.[9] Broadly, but not absolutely, policy was little affected by academic work, and direct engagement and effect in other areas was barely noticeable.[10]

However, this started to change, in the late 1990s, with greater openness to advice and, in particular, to informing policy with evidence. UK research councils, responding to government preferences, began to curate research programmes to address emerging international security questions. In this context, a number of programmes provide a body of material to consider in this present section. Although we recognise that this is a limited selection of research and could be seen as a distorted sample of all the research on international affairs being undertaken, in that period, we note that there are two strong reasons to focus on this body of material. First, it identifies clear sets of projects, delineating a sample to consider, rather than more haphazardly trying to identify different pieces of research that might inform our study. Secondly, reinforcing the first point, these are the kinds of major, funded research that might be expected to make a difference; that was, no doubt, part of the thinking in seeking to fund research in specific fields. For the present purpose, we have considered three bodies of programmatic research: New Security Challenges (NSC — which had

---

9 Freedman's memo can be found at https://webarchive.nationalarchives.gov.uk/ 20160512100735/http://www.iraqinquiry.org.uk/media/42664/freedman-powell-letter.pdf available at 29 November 2019. Freedman had been appointed to the UK's first ever Strategic Defence Review; the other two academics were Colin Gray and James Gow.

10 We should note that, in this context, we are focusing on the policy world and closely related practice. This limits the discussion in some ways, in principle, as other aspects of impact are not explored. This makes the task more manageable, however — and also reflects how impact has been seen within POLIS. We discuss in Chapters 2 and 8 the extent to which this limits an overall understanding of impact by excluding cultural, legal or other forms of impact.

three iterations), Religion and Society, and Global Uncertainties, each of which involved a mix of research councils, but with the Economic and Social Research Council (ESRC) leading on the first and last, and the Arts and Humanities Research Council (AHRC) leading on the middle one.

This body of research revealed notable potential for impact being developed, even though research funders had yet to introduce the impact focus. There was the prospect of considerable 'world-leading' research impact, with then fairly novel emergence of multi- and interdisciplinary research. The three NSC programmes were led ably by Stuart Croft. These three programmes were intended to change the frame of research in international studies to address a perceived lack of funding for areas such as international security, on one side, and to bring new researchers into the realm of security research to boost interdisciplinary research, on the other. And all of this was done with the aim of generating research to produce knowledge and understanding for a rapidly changing, post-Cold War environment for the UK.

Without doubt, some NSC-funded projects clearly yielded useful research. These included work led by Funmi Olonisakin on youth exclusion, militancy and violence in West Africa, which resulted in recognition that the age range covered by the label 'youth' needed to be extended by the Economic Community of West African States (ECOWAS), with significant impact indicated by the organisation and its members adopting this change in 2009 to capture the full range of 'youth' in their activities. This even found its way into a REF2014 impact case study, deemed to be one of the top 20 by one development organisation.[11] From the Global Uncertainties Programme, David Willetts, then Secretary of State responsible for universities, used the example of Theo Farrell's research focused on the UK military campaign in Afghanistan. This prompted the UK Government's Stabilisation Unit and the British Army to invite him to assist in reviewing British operations in Helmand Province, which contributed to organisational reform, including restructuring of UK inter-agency operations. This was research translating into British defence and security lesson learning, which also fed into the 2010 UK Strategic Defence and Security Review.[12] While

11 See www.ukcdr.org.uk/what-we-do/the-impact-of-uk-research-for-development/ available at 29 November 2019.
12 Rt. Hon. David Willetts MP, 'Our Hi-Tech Future', Oral Statement to Parliament, 4 January 2012, available at www.gov.uk/government/speeches/our-hi-tech-future--2 at 4 February 2020.

the Religion and Society Programme was not focused on international security, per se, being intended to address legal and social change involving religion and equality, there were strong security aspects to the research conducted under the Programme, including the excellent work by Basia Spalek,[13] on partnership and counter-terrorism, as well as the importance of faith among Muslim police officers, and also the core work by Programme Director Linda Woodhead, whose study for the new Equalities and Human Rights Commission informed, if not introduced, religion as a fifth pillar of the British equalities framework — developments that, while inherently important, also had implications for tackling terrorism and for international security.[14]

Yet, despite the promise and some signs of research making a difference, these programmes were often a disappointment, most notably the last of three NSC programmes, New Security Challenges Radicalisation and Violence (NSCRV). NSCRV was the most clearly intended to generate useful research, in particular, for the UK FCO, which contributed financially to the programme and sought to benefit from research findings. The NSCRV programme was disappointing because the quality and relevance of projects was lacking, which did not result in evidence that government could use. The FCO hoped to generate empirical assessment of particular places that it could not obtain from its own capabilities. Understandably, perhaps, researchers probably 'did what they wanted to do anyway', continuing their avenues of research and not delivering to order.

One way in which the programmes clearly made a difference, however, was to the character of international security studies, generating significant multi- and interdisciplinary research. Even if leaving out traditional international security, for the most part, this significantly widened the span of researchers and disciplines involved.

13 Basia Spalek, Salwa el-Awa, Laura Zahra McDonald, *Police-Muslim Engagement and Partnerships for the Purposes of Counter-Terrorism: an examination*, Summary Report, Birmingham: University of Birmingham and AHRC Religion and Society Programme, 18 November 2008; *Community Partnerships to Prevent Violent Extremism: The UK Experience*, Presentation, International Association of Chiefs of Police 118th Annual Conference and Exposition, 25 October 2011; Basia Spalek and Lynn Davies with Laura Zahra McDonald, *Key Evaluation Findings of the West Midlands [WM] 1-2-1 Mentoring Scheme*, Birmingham: University of Birmingham, 2010.

14 Linda Woodhead with Rebecca Catto, '*Religion or belief': Identifying Issues and Priorities*, Equality and Human Rights Commission Research Report 48, Manchester: Equality and Human Rights Commission, 2009. Religion was added to the four existing categories in which equalities legislation and policy applied: race, gender, sex and disability.

From more than 40 NSC projects, no more than six involved those who had a profile for conducting research on more conventional aspects of international security. Moreover, perhaps only four projects related, in some way, to traditional security studies concerns. Three of these four focused on terrorism, perhaps unsurprisingly, given the context of the 9/11 terrorist attacks by al-Qa'ida (and religion and jihadism would become themes in the research programmes, notably Religion and Society, with religious knowledge essential in fighting violent ideology, and religious convictions providing strong motivations to fight violence[15]). This left one project with one recognised international security expert considering a traditional defence topic — involving Terry Terriff on military institutional learning. A similar pattern featured with the Global Uncertainties Fellowships, where only one project from 15 clearly addressed a conventional security concern — Theo Farrell's study, mentioned above, while another two addressed new dimensions of security, but with established international security scholars.[16] As well as broadening the range of scholars engaged in the field, these programmes also expanded the range and types of methods used in international studies, notably the adoption and inclusion of social research methods previously more associated with sociology, or anthropology — combined with other methods and adapted for use.

There was clearly benefit and value in strategic programmes with a focus on international security. New agendas could be addressed and set, and frames were re-set. Yet, the outcomes were uneven, both in terms of coverage and findings. Whilst there were a number of disappointments, there were clearly also examples of high quality, which had the potential for impact — and, as shown in some examples above, did so. It was also evident that, sometimes, research simply captured a *zeitgeist*,[17] or that engagement and research process simply had an effect.[18] Yet, two clouds cast a shadow over this positive depiction. One was, as suggested,

---

15 In this context, 'jihad' is a problematic and contested area, with some claiming to act in the name of Islam by perpetrating violence invoking it, while others, promoting the faith, use the term — which approximately means 'just struggle' — to oppose the use of violence.

16 Professor Sir L.D. Freedman of King's College London, for 'Strategic scripts for the 21st century'; Professor N.J. Wheeler, Aberystwyth University, for 'The challenges to trust-building in a nuclear world'.

17 This reflects a comment to the authors that often research outcomes and impact may simply be a matter of serendipity — it can just be the right time for a piece of research to be done, or to have some effect.

18 It was the process of engagement itself and contact with particular researchers that made a difference, as noted above.

that the extent of potentially world-leading impact did not appear to be commensurate with funding through these programmes. Secondly, even where there was potentially significant impact, this seemed unfulfilled. In REF2014, performance was seemingly below par, with no 100 per cent 4* submissions. Even in terms of the uneven record in the field, the outcome was relatively weak, the issue we identified at the start of this enquiry and which we address in the final section of this chapter.

Research impact 2014 — Politics and International Studies

As noted already, no submission in Politics and International Studies gained a full house of world-leading scores for impact in REF2014. This is partly reflective of the uneven pattern of research findings and impact emerging from major strategic funding programmes, as discussed in the previous section. Yet, it is, at the same time, also an outcome that occurred despite the quality evident from certain parts of that funding, which suggested that there could have been greater impact than was recognised in the REF results. Of course, a further factor in reflection on this topic is that much research could be conducted away from major strategic programmes, or without specific external funding — as was, in practice, often the case. Yet, the very benchmark of quality found in those programmes — self-described as world-leading research by the research councils — ought also to have correlated more strongly with world-leading examples of impact. In this last section of the chapter, we consider the top performing submissions in Politics and International Studies in REF2014, in particular, to explore what constituted the most highly evaluated body of impact in that exercise and if this can offer any further elucidation on why politics and international studies failed in REF2014.

A handful of politics and international studies submissions had creditable ratings in the 60s range, including the LSE (61.4), Leeds (66.7) and our own King's College London (63.6), and three others precisely on the 60 mark (Bradford, Strathclyde and York). All but four of the others fell well below that '2:1' level (to borrow from the traditional British first degree classification system). Those four were the top submissions. Three of them, Oxford, Essex and Sheffield, were clearly above the 'first class' 70 mark (to continue the degree classification analogy), with one, Keele, sitting right on the 70 boundary.

In the remainder of this chapter, we consider these most highly rated cases in politics and international studies.

The Keele submission was small, entailing just two case studies. One of them, which included drafting the UK Green Party's election manifesto, as well as introducing the notion of 'environmental citizenship', and also involved supporting quotation', read as a strong and convincing example of research that made a difference. The second study, on international human rights and issues of hate speech, seemed less convincing, though indicating considerable engagement and respect, with some impact surely emerging from it. But, the impression, overall, was of a very good, but not wholly convincing, submission. In this respect, this seemed to reflect the unevenness of wider politics and international studies impact achievements: sometimes excellent, but not consistently so.

Two of the Sheffield studies focus around the research of one scholar, in particular, Matthew Flinders. One, on engaging citizens in politics, shows clear capacity building, in developing courses with the Houses of Parliament. It also made claims about public engagement and discourse, and making a three-part series for BBC Radio 4 with a suggested audience reach of 1.7 million, that could well have impressed, even if this did not completely fit the official definitions of impact, as discussed in Chapters 2 and 3. The second Flinders example, *Reforming Public Bodies*, had extensive and impressive quotation, including the judgement of the Chair of the House of Commons Select Committee on Public Administration that '... many of the actual recommendations made by the committee are actually explicitly linked to either his written submission of evidence or to points he made when appearing in front of the committee.' This kind of quotation left no doubt that there had been effect — and, complemented by rich detail on work in Parliament and with other parts of government, a strong sense of value. It might be that two case studies framed around one scholar diminished the overall rating. This suggestion is aired because unverifiable anecdote and gossip suggested a belief and understanding among scholars that the sub-panel had somehow seen two studies framed around one individual as involving duplication, one case undermining the other. The third in the Sheffield set was framed around a different individual, Andrew Geddes. *Reshaping the Global Policy Agenda on Environmental Change and Migration* involved research developing more sophisticated understanding of migration in relation to environmental change, which was used directly by two UK government departments, as well as the World Bank. It also entailed wide engagement and, no doubt, wider impact, as well as significant news media coverage. As with the first two studies, there was evidence of strong and unquestionable impact.

The Essex submission contained two studies. One focused on a very familiar figure to viewers of British elections, Sir Anthony King, and the role his research played in reforming the BBC's approach to, and coverage of, its component nations, including notably increasing and improving news coverage of the devolved institutions, such as the Scottish Parliament and the Welsh Assembly. The study showed that the BBC Trust had welcomed the research and acted upon it, making repeated references to the difference King's work had made. The second Essex study was on human rights and the quality of democracy, research geared to evaluating the latter, in effect. While less emphatic, perhaps, the evidence was clear that the 28-member inter-governmental organisation the International Institute for Democracy and Electoral Assistance (International IDEA) had benefited from the research, which underpinned a range of resources used by the orga-nisation in training and evaluation, for which Todd Landman at Essex had been the lead author, drawing on the research, and which had been translated into four languages to ensure its extended use. We discuss these cases again, briefly, and the possibility that they might be regarded as world leading, in the Conclusion.

The far larger Oxford submission — one of the largest in the field — had nine case studies, making its achievement as the highest-scoring submission remarkable. Space precludes discussion of them all. But, a key observation is that this collection was uneven, in some respects. Some of the studies are clearly as good as could be, such as that framed around Richard Caplan's work on benchmarking UN peacebuilding, which densely reflects stunning contributions to identifying issues and offering solutions, with a key briefing note underpinning develop-ments, including a UN handbook. Also impressive was the study around Jennifer Welsh and her research influence on the UN and the 'Responsibility to Protect' doctrine's interpretation and use to prevent mass atrocities. With another study embracing various positions the eminent Adam Roberts had held and a collection of bits and pieces of claimed impact through membership of bodies, the suspicion might emerge that the REF Politics and International Studies sub-panel might have lost sight of demanding strong evidence and clear effect, and been persuaded more by standing and reputation in a set of engagements — though no doubt having significant impact, as anyone aware of Roberts and his work would recognise. But, that suspicion is made stronger if the study on shaping ethics in Western militaries is addressed.

Framed around another beacon in the field, David Rodin, this was a case study that surely begged questions. While his work clearly had some capacity-building influence, with books used by military academies, it was surely not the only material used, and claims to influence through occasional lectures at the UK Defence Academy, notable as they are, might raise eyebrows among the many others, including the dedicated academics from King's College London who, as academic providers to the Defence Academy, translate research into effect all the time (but, curiously, this was not something considered by King's in its own approach). Most curiously, a press report used to support a claim about rules of engagement for the British armed forces in Afghanistan in 2007, makes no reference to Rodin, or Oxford — and even includes a statement that the rules of engagement had not been changed, according the UK Ministry of Defence. To compound this apparent weakness, the newspaper report itself indicates that whatever tactical change had occurred had made British troops more vulnerable. It is hard not to imagine that Rodin's excellent work on ethics and the use of force, and his reputation, had left a greater impression than the material in the study itself. Of course, we cannot know how the sub-panel handled this — and we cannot know the extent to which that which we would view as apparent weakness in this study was perhaps responsible for Oxford's not gaining 100 per cent at the top level.

Having reviewed the best-performing submissions in REF2014, against the background of impact in international affairs more globally and also the targeted research funded by UK research councils ahead of REF2014, it is evident that there was both a desire for and accomplishment of impact, and also some major differences made, alongside potential emerging from research council programmes, even before the official agenda emerged. Yet, the record was uneven: potential was missed, or impact was simply missing. REF2014 reflected this. Not only did no submission gain 100 per cent 4*, but also examination of some highly scored submissions posed questions, potentially, about some of the sub-panel's judgements. Generally, impact was an uneven business. This point is reflected in the submissions that gained the highest outcomes in the REF exercise — and perhaps in the fact that no submission in the Unit of Assessment gained 100 per cent at that world-leading level.

The failure to gain a full house at that level might simply be deemed to be the way of things — it simply is not possible to produce a 100 per cent outcome. Yet, as noted from the start of the book, the evidence is that it was possible to gain a 100 per cent 4* grading. To understand more about what achieving that level entails, the following three chapters will investigate the qualities and characteristics of world-leading research, presenting our own findings about the qualities common to top-level case studies in Chapters 6 and 7, and, before that, setting up the issue and considering other research with the same aim, albeit of a different character, in Chapter 5.

5   4* Impact — world leading

A key question for many researchers and their universities is how to maximise impact — or, more specifically, in the context of research excellence evaluations, 'how can we get the highest rating'? This was an important question, as not only a sense of achievement and standing, but also money followed (albeit, only to the institution). This mattered. While much emphasis was placed on 'outputs' (that is, for the most part, publications of some kind), in the UK REF2014, a good impact story was more valuable.

With researchers required to submit four pieces as standard, in that iteration of the exercise, even if all four were deemed to be of 4* quality, that would be some way short of the average value of £46,311 for a top-rated impact case study (ICS).[1] It was little known and less appreciated that one world-leading 4* output was certainly worth less than a quarter of an ICS, and might more likely be worth around perhaps one sixth of an equivalent ICS. The ratio of 4.37 outputs to one impact case study was reported by the highly respected LSE Impact Blog in a piece by the equally highly respected Simon Kerridge. However, this figure was not related specifically to the top level, world-leading category alone, but an average across quality levels. However, while it is almost impossible to know exactly what the relative values of outputs and ICSs was, our research indicates that the ratio could well be over 1 to 6 for 4* material in REF2014. In one of the concrete examples we were able to consider confidentially, which is very useful for simple illustration of the ratio found generally in necessarily limited

---

1 Mark Reed and Simon Kerridge, 'How much was an impact case study worth in the UK Research Excellence Framework?' *Fast Track Impact*, 1 February 2017, available at www.fasttrackimpact.com/single-post/2017/02/01/How-much-was-an-impact-case-study-worth-in-the-UK-Research-Excellence-Framework available at 29 November 2019.

data, a 4* output was worth, on average, £10,624 and an impact case study £68,962.[2] Where this was known and understood, it simply added to the quest for the Holy Grail of 4* impact.

How to get 4* impact, in the UK context of REF, became an important question — but, outside the UK context, where perhaps different standards or no actual rating existed, it was an increasingly important factor. What was world-leading, top-level research impact — and how could it be achieved, both in practice, and, with any eye on appreciation and pecuniary return, in evaluation exercises? Surprisingly, few scholars, individually or institutionally, paid attention to this significant question (as noted in the Introduction). In part, this might have been a matter of being overwhelmed — where would anyone start with almost 7,000 impact case studies in REF2014, across 36 Units of Assessment? As it turned out, there were ways. One was serendipitously and unintentionally brought to us. Another was developed by Mark Reed, at Newcastle University, and his colleagues, who were very explicitly interested in the question of what made top-scoring impact in REF2014 — and what could make it in REF2021. This was pellucid in the name of Reed's spin-off company and website: Fast Track Impact.

We discuss the Newcastle and Fast Track research, in the course of this chapter, and present our own in the subsequent two chapters, with all three chapters to be read as a whole, to gain fuller understanding, both of what might constitute 4* impact and also of how to consider the apparent underperformance of international studies. While we cannot promise a 'how to ...' kit (as our caveats below and in Chapter 7 make clear), we do provide clear insights into the elements associated with top-level research impact. The two approaches are quite distinct, yet perfectly complementary. Both are completely focused on the UK REF exercise. This raises some issues, which we address in the first part of the chapter, below, where it is important to understand that, while the empirical material with which we deal is UK-focused and could seem parochial, it is not: the findings and their significance resonate globally. For this reason, before we critically expose the discourse research of Mark Reed, the first section in this chapter gives some context on the UK REF, on possible limitations that this might

2 Simon Kerridge, 'Hitting the QR sweet spot: will new REF2021 rules lead to a different kind of game-playing?' available at https://blogs.lse.ac.uk/impactofsocialsciences/2018/03/07/hitting-the-qr-sweet-spot-will-the-new-ref2021-rules-lead-to-a-different-kind-of-game-playing/ available at 29 November 2019. We are grateful to Louise Atkins for her immense insight and help to understand the funding information we have used here.

bring — meaning both the British focus and also the nature of the evaluation process, and establishes our approach.

REF in the UK and approach

To some extent, anyone not familiar with the REF in the UK may already have some idea about it from earlier parts of the book. However, this section offers more information about that exercise, as the context for the material presented later in this chapter and also to allow us to flag some issues and limitations.[3] We will do so to set the scope of our study and to allow comment on questions of methodology and approach. On this basis, it should be clear how the analysis might best be understood. Thus, in the present section, we will first outline the essentials of the REF exercise and then introduce the analysis that follows.

Aside from documents produced by the various bodies responsible for REF and many an internet or email comment and odd opinion pieces in the press, surprisingly little has been written about it and impact. As we noted in the Introduction, the reference points for writing this book were few and far between — the work of Mark Reed and his colleagues (discussed below), that of Jonathan Grant and his colleagues, and the inspirational and pathfinding volume by Gemma Derrick, which informed parts of Chapter 2. That chapter also contained references to some articles on aspects of impact. But, the real history of REF has yet to be written. The following paragraphs offer a sketch of what that history might include.

The Research Excellence Framework (REF) is a national audit of university and equivalent research in the UK, as indicated in Chapter 1. It is funded and required by the various core funding bodies for higher education and research. As of 2018, these were the Department for the Economy NI (Northern Ireland), the Higher Education Funding Council for Wales (HEFCW), Research England and the Scottish Funding Council. Though each was the renamed version of its predecessors, these were the titles, following a reorganisation and re-branding, that also brought them together with the various UK research funding councils under the auspices of the overarching UKRI

---

3 We are grateful to one of the peer reviewers of the book, who suggested that we offer some context and history regarding REF, to make sure that both the potential significance and the possible limitations of our analysis might be appreciated. This is particularly relevant to the discussion below regarding the possible limitations of analysis stemming only from REF impact case studies.

(UK Research and Innovation). Prior to the first iteration of REF, in 2014, a cognate audit, called the Research Assessment Exercise (RAE) ran four times, in 1992, 1996, 2001 and 2008. Whatever the label, and whatever the detail, these were all accountability exercises, where the funding bodies, on behalf of the UK government which provides most research money and all direct, core research funding while broadly leaving the academy to get on with its business of research and education, wanted a sense of the 'value' gained for the investment.

Through all its iterations, the assessment of research quality has been carried out as a peer exercise, in line with the principles of academic autonomy and non-interference, whether political or bureaucratic (even if an entirely pure version of this could never actually be achieved, given inherent biases and human nature). Organised into main panels and sub-panels, working with funding council guidelines, these peer panels, comprising established researchers from the variety of areas, disciplines and fields in which research was conducted, read the voluminous submissions, met, evaluated them, met again, and produced a final assessment for each one. There could not be a sub-panel for every last small field, with the consequences that not all research could fit easily and comfortably into the framework; and the precise number and designation of sub-panels changed with each new edition of the research exercise — the Politics and International Studies unit started as number 42, in 1992, but by REF 2021 would be number 19, with the overall number of units shrinking from 72, at that first point, to just 34 for 2021. In the time of the RAE, prior to 2008, sub-panels would simply give an overall rating, having evaluated a mass of material, including thousands of publications. So, in Politics and International Studies, for example, in the 1996 and 2001 iterations of the exercise, the same four units received the highest outcome (5*) in each exercise: Sheffield, Essex, Oxford, and King's College London (though in the latter, the University of Wales Aberystwyth, now University of Aberystwyth, also received that top grade).[4]

More variegation was introduced with REF, with units being given a profile, rather than one simple score, and that profile was rendered as

4 In the original RAE, 5 had been the top rating. 5* was introduced in 1996 to generate greater discrimination at the top end of the scales. Through the first three versions of the RAE, Essex and King's College London achieved the top level in each exercise. With the introduction of profiles in RAE2008 (a practice continued with the transformation into the REF), differentiation immediately emerged — albeit with some discussion and controversy.

a percentage of the submission, in each of three sections, at a certain level. The three sections were outputs, impact and environment, with the first most heavily weighted. There were five levels at which a submitting unit could be scored in each of these categories: 1–4* (1–4 stars) and unclassified. The different star levels correlated to different levels of achievement — world leading, internationally excellent, recognised internationally, nationally recognised, unclassified. Each of these levels had a specific definition:[5]

Four star — 4*:

> Quality that is world leading in terms of originality, significance and rigour.

Three star — 3*:

> Quality that is internationally excellent in terms of originality, significance and rigour but which falls short of the highest standards of excellence.

Two star — 2*:

> Quality that is recognised internationally in terms of originality, significance and rigour.

One star — 1*:

> Quality that is recognised nationally in terms of originality, significance and rigour.

Unclassified:

> Quality that falls below the standard of nationally recognised work. Or work which does not meet the published definition of research for the purposes of this assessment.

These overall categories applied to the three elements in the profile — outputs, impact and environment (where the first of these referred to

---

5 *REF2014 Expert Panels — Assessment Criteria and Level Descriptions* available at www.ref.ac.uk/2014/panels/assessmentcriteriaandleveldefinitions/ at 5 December 2019.

Table 5.1 University of Sheffield

	4*	3*	2*	1*	U
Overall	52	37	10	1	0
Outputs	43.1	43.1	12.1	1.7	0
Impact	73.3	26.7	0	0	0
Environment	62.5	25.0	12.5	0	0

(Source: *REF2014 — Results and Submissions*, Unit of Assessment 21 available at https://results.ref.ac.uk/(S(4y2qsu2ekbcqlvfw3ieebv4j))/Results/ByUoa/21 at 5 December 2019)

Note
FTE Category A staff: 18.00.

publications, in the main, and other ways in which research was reported and shown, and the last referred to a statement written to describe the unit, its context and its approach to research). For impact, given its peculiar character, the definition was recast to have a focus on the 'reach' and 'significance' of claimed impacts. In this context, the 4* level was labelled 'outstanding', in terms of these features, 3*, 2* and 1* were 'very considerable', 'considerable' and 'recognised but modest', respectively. The unclassified category embraced things that just did not qualify — that were not underpinned by excellent research, where the claimed impact was not eligible — perhaps wrong in terms of when it occurred, and claims where the impact could not be discerned at all or was so little, in terms of reach and significance, that it did not register. In practice, these descriptors were applied to 'reach' and 'significance' jointly, not treating these aspects separately. Rather, there was an 'overall view', with simply the 'oomph' of a case study being gauged, rather than fine tuning grades for either of the measures. This included an assessment of whether a given unit's approach to impact, as expressed in the contextual template statement required, was 'conducive to achieving impacts of "reach and significance".'[6]

In each category, at each level, a percentage figure would be given, reflecting the sub-panel's judgement on the proportion of material submitted at that particular level. So, in REF2014, rather than one overall score (although, in different ways, one of these could be produced — and, of course, they were), each submission was given a profile in a 15-box grid of scores: three category rows and five proportion columns. For example, Table 5.1 shows how the profile looked for Sheffield.

6 *REF2014 Expert Panels — Assessment Criteria and Level Descriptions* available at www.ref.ac.uk/2014/panels/assessmentcriteriaandleveldefinitions/ at 5 December 2019.

Table 5.2 University of Essex

	4*	3*	2*	1*	U
Overall	68	19	12	1	0
Outputs	59.4	23.9	15.7	1	0
Impact	80	10	10	0	0
Environment	87.5	12.5	0	0	0

(Source: *REF2014 — Results and Submissions*, Unit of Assessment 21 available at https://results.ref.ac.uk/(S(4y2qsu2ekbcqlvfw3ieebv4j))/Results/ByUoa/21 at 5 December 2019).

Note
FTE Category A staff: 29.95.

And Table 5.2 shows the profile for Essex.

Whereas Sheffield and Essex had been awarded the same, single rating in the past, the finer-grained approach separated them clearly in REF2014, giving them different overall ratings.

The impact section was a novelty, introduced with REF2014. The definition, issues around it and the general approach to it were discussed in Chapter 2. Our focus on impact evidently makes that part of the REF process our interest. This REF-centric approach to impact raises some issues that we cannot fully address, but, it is none the less worth indicating them.

As we have shown in earlier parts of the book, impact existed before REF was created and has wider senses that are not necessarily embraced by this accountability process. While some of the questions regarding the wider scope of impact were dealt with in Chapter 2, we must be aware that it is possible, at least, that the material in our archive, that is, the REF2014 published profiles and submissions, has a particular character, or has been regarded in a particular way. Either of these would mean that the discrete selections of ICSs on which both the discourse investigation developed by Reed, Reichard and colleagues, which we present in the following section, and our own analysis, in the chapters after that, could reflect a distorted, perhaps limited, version of impact. In that sense, our examination of world-leading research impact might require qualification: it is an examination of world-leading research impact *of a certain kind — the kind that, axiomatically, is defined as impact of a world-leading quality by REF peer review panels.*

To be clear, while the empirical research presented here is limited to the UK REF material we have identified, this in no way means that the analysis is only relevant to the UK — it certainly is not, as we indicated in the Introduction and could be inferred from Chapter 3 — and nor does it mean that our generalised findings are not generalisable beyond the REF or UK contexts. However, given the selective nature of the REF process, we have to be aware that, while without doubt our research is wholly valid in the context of REF considerations, it is possible that the sample used might be a skewed and distorted segment of a wider category of impact. There is the implicit assumption in our approach that the analysis has general relevance in the realm of impact and that it is likely that our analysis about the characteristics of world-leading research is generalisable. However, without the opportunity to test this assumption comparatively against a set of non-REF impact material, it might be that our findings would not hold in some other, unknown, impact arena. Without that kind of comparison, there is a theoretical limitation that might apply. Indeed, it is certain that the REF process and the demands it makes for impact to be presented with a certain shape, according to the five sections on the ICS template (summary, under-pinning research, references to research, details of impact and supporting references for impact described) could also be — indeed, almost certainly was — a limitation on the scope of research impact. The extent to which this could be the case, in our view, is moderately small, given the variety or impacts and routes to impact to be found within the constraints of the REF process and its template for presenting research impact — recalling the more than 3,000 pathways that Grant and his colleagues identified within the REF2014 impact case studies. It seems likely to us that the kind of impact represented in the REF crucible is reflective and re-presentative of research impacts more widely. However, inevitably, our analysis (and also that of Reed *et al.*) is focused on those case studies and cannot escape the bounds of the way they are framed and written for the purpose of REF evaluation — and so, while confident in the research, its validity overall and what might be taken by some as generalisable lessons (though we caution against doing this too naïvely), it is important to be aware that, were the same research impacts presented in a different context, for a different purpose, some of the characteristics we identify might not feature, or might do so only in some modified form (and this, again, we would add, applies in the same way to the research by Reed *et al.*, based on REF ICSs, that we introduce below). Our acknowledging these limitations, in the end, does not, we judge, in any way undermine the analysis we offer in the following chapters.[7] Before that, we pave the

---

7 This tallies, we are content to note, with the view of the peer reviewer of our work, who suggested that we should reflexively discuss the nature of REF and how the peculiarities of that process might affect our general analysis.

way with a critical exposition of the quite different, but complementary, and immensely valuable research on high-scoring ICSs by Reed, Reichard and their colleagues.

Discourse and high-scoring impact

The first attempt to investigate what constituted a successful impact case study in REF2014 was made by Mark Reed, along with some colleagues at Newcastle and elsewhere. Alongside this, he set up a spin-off consultancy company to provide training and advice as a service, and established, as part of that, the very useful Fast Track Impact website, which became an engaging source of impact information, as well as the home for presenting the impact research. That research was important in identifying how language was used and made — or at least, represented — a difference between high- and low-scoring ICSs.[8] Reed produced valuable research, working closely, in particular, with a PhD student (initially), Bella Reichard — who became the lead researcher and author in published academic work.[9] While rich and diverse, in many respects, the research was focused on a bald question: what makes a 4* impact case study?[10]

Reed and Reichard's research used 190 ICSs that had 'extreme' impact profiles in REF2014, meaning that they were either completely towards the high-scoring end, or completely at the opposite end. So, where a submission was evaluated as, say, 90 per cent 4* and 10 per cent 3*, it would count in the upper cohort; where it was 90 per cent 2* and 10 per cent 1*, by contrast, it would be in the lower one. Of course, the precise percentage balance would not necessarily be the same. But, a clear division between a high-scoring sample and a low-scoring sample could be made. This provided the basis for discourse analysis that probed the type of language that could be associated either with high-scoring ICSs, or with low-scoring ones. In this analysis, the researchers looked for phrases that occurred

---

8 It might be recalled, from the discussion in Chapter 2, that one of the features in early research on impact — and issues with softer versions of impact, or non-impact — was also discussion about language, with more active language, in effect, more capturing impact.

9 Bellla Reichard, Mark S. Reed, J. Chubb, G. Hall, L. Jowett and A. Peart, 'Pathways to a top-scoring impact case study', *Palgrave Communications* (in press at time of writing).

10 See www.fasttrackimpact.com/single-post/2017/12/19/What-makes-a-4-research-impact-case-study-for-REF2021.

more frequently with one category, or the other. This would offer a picture of language more likely to be associated with high- or low-scoring ICSs.

Not wholly unsurprisingly, high-scoring accounts were found to be well written and easy to understand. The selection of words was significant — so far as possible avoiding research jargon and specialist terms (which have to be unavoidable sometimes, of course), and choosing direct and plain speech. This was especially notable regarding the underpinning research sections, where the temptations to use specialist language could be greatest. The key advantage of using language this way was that it ensured that cause and effect were lucidly set out, thus making the impact case strongly. Low-scoring accounts failed in these key challenges. They tended to be opaquely framed with academic language, both of the more technical, or abstruse, kind and also of the woolly, or cautious, kind — 'in relation to', 'in terms of' or 'the ways in which' padded out the studies, and, often, the research and impact were found to be obscured by the language. It was possible that genuine and notable impact was lost behind the unnecessary, unfocused and verbose language. However, it was, perhaps, more likely that feeble language used in contrast to the strong language in the better-performing ICSs reflected, as the panel judgements would suggest, weak examples of impact.

The key finding in this research was that successful ICSs had clearly articulated benefits to specific groups, and provided evidence of significance and reach (these last two points, evidently, reflecting the REF criteria for impact). Some 84 per cent of high-scoring ICSs were found to have indicated significance and reach of specific benefits. Phrases indicating specific groups and (or) reach, or significance, included 'in England' and 'millions of ...', 'the government', 'the department of', 'for the first time, the BBC ...' In all of this, phrases of clear attribution and specific definition of focus were commonly found — attribution to specific research and attribution to named, or defined, beneficiaries.

By contrast, 32 per cent of low-scoring submissions referred to what might be summarised as 'pathways' to impact — so the dissemination and engagement activity from which making a difference might emerge, but without clearly saying what difference, if any, had actually been made. Here the language used was weaker and vaguer. Terms used included 'a number' and 'a range', rather than giving a concrete specific number to indicate the scale of impact. The research-impact nexus was portrayed in language that lacked solid references — 'work in', 'has informed', 'through', 'the relationship between', 'research into', or 'research project.' There is, of course, nothing wrong, as such, with these terms, but they require more firmly drawn definition — for instance, not 'research project', but 'X [named] research project.' Similarly, and in some ways slightly more problematically, terms such as 'locally', 'in local', and 'the north' were associated with low-scoring ICSs. This is problematic because it could suggest that, for example, 'local' is not as big as 'national', or 'international', and so the word is a measure of a lack of reach. This is wrong, however. The problem is the absence of solid references to the specific locality involved. So, a stronger submission might have said 'in the locality of X [named]', where the empirical detail of named places takes away any sense of vagueness. Research impact, where it occurs, affects real people, places and organisations. One individual could be the full extent of an impact, theoretically, in which case its reach and significance would be great, and complete. But, the individual would need to be identified and the scope of the case delineated. Similarly, a 'local' benefit should not be represented in an amorphous manner with just that word, but, for example, specific 'local' amenities, services, organisations or named, or defined, communities, should be the object of impact. The 'local' is not capable of benefiting, whereas, for instance, an allotment association, or a set of them, might be.

To some extent, this valuable research simply confirms that which good understanding would expect. Certainly, from experience of supporting the development of ICSs, there is something familiar in the commitment of researchers to their particular versions of research and their preferred language, couched in caution and hedging claims, when the use of strong, active verbs is appropriate and specifying detail is required. The Reed, Reichard *et al.* research certainly points to the strong need for clearly expressed narratives that provide concrete information, with full attribution and evidence. Of course, the thing that all of this assumes is that the impact claimed is actually there. All the good writing in the world will have little purpose if there is no genuine story to tell. Indeed, it might well be — as Derrick found in her research (described in Chapter 2) — that where there is an excellent impact story, it will be perfectly evident and, almost — but only almost — write itself. That could well be the reason that the features of discourse identified in the Fast Track research are there to be identified: when the case is clear and strong, those telling it and owning it would find it hard not to give it good expression. Certainly, there can be no doubting that the research on language and discourse in high-scoring (3* and 4*) ICSs in REF2014, reported here, is highly significant and should be grasped by anyone seeking to understand the characteristics of world-leading research, certainly in the context of research excellence evaluation. However, language is not the only feature of high-quality impact ICSs and it may not be enough only to focus on this single aspect. Moreover, the discourse analysis does not isolate the very top level, as such — the 4* standard, in terms of the UK REF. In the following two chapters, we offer a discrete, but complementary, analysis focused on the characteristics of impact at that standard.

6 The eight characteristics of world-leading, 4* impact: 1–5

In the present chapter, we offer our own research on impact case studies we know to have been rated at the highest level in the Research Excellence Framework REF2014. Building on the exposition of Mark Reed and his colleagues' discourse study, presented in Chapter 5, on the qualities of high-calibre impact, we present the results of our close-reading analysis of the 111 world-leading impact case studies we identified. In the course of the two chapters, we outline eight elements common to 4* impact case studies (ICS): 1. long-term research and impact context; 2. quality/significant research funding; 3. clear engagement/an embedded role in implementation/researcher-practitioner unity; 4. resource/financial commitment to impact; 5. quotes as evidence and presentation; 6. breadth/range/multiplicity/cumulative effect; 7. creating something new/transformative for beneficiaries; 8. news media engagement and public engagement. In the following chapter, we set out characteristics 6 to 8. In the remainder of this chapter, we indicate the first five.

Identifying world-leading impact

Our analysis began after Gow attended a presentation by Dr. Steven Hill, Head of Research Policy at the Higher Education Funding Council for England (HEFCE) (as both his post and organisation were titled at the time) at the TCCE (The Capital Cultural Exchange) on 10 July 2017. That presentation, to a largely arts-focused mixture of academics and practitioners, highlighted 'good' examples of arts-related ICSs from REF2014. In the course of this talk, Steven Hill incidentally showed a slide indicating that an institution submitted to Unit of Assessment (UoA) 35 (Music, Drama, Dance and Performing Arts) had achieved 100 per cent on Impact in 2014. The information was not the purpose of the slide, as it sat alongside points about two other institutions, which institutions had not achieved this complete success (even though it is likely that the presenter was aware of that which he was showing and, even, offering a more or less hidden sign to anyone who noticed it). Gow subsequently had a conversation with Hill, which set in train this project.

Following this, a process of identifying instances of 100 per cent on Impact in REF2014 was undertaken, starting with the initial 10 found in UoA 35. The project involved close reading of ICSs — empirical critical evaluation of documents to see if particular, common features could be identified. This process first produced an initial study of ten 4* ICSs presented in REF2014 — impact case studies that were judged to be world leading in that exercise. After preliminary analysis, and preparing a short paper, without relating his observations and identification of eight features common to the decade of case studies, Gow invited Redwood (who was, at that point, Impact Research Associate in the School of Security Studies at King's College London, assisting Gow) to consider the same ten ICSs. He independently arrived at almost exactly the same inferences, observing the same features detailed below.

A further six instances of 4* ICSs were identified and analysed. The original draft paper was, then, supplemented by analysis of these six further ICSs, as we continued to explore and seek to identify other 100 per cent 4* ICSs. The additional six case studies showed no anomalies and confirmed the consistency of the preliminary analysis. On the basis of those 16 ICSs, we were able to produce an interim draft paper that was presented several times, including to colleagues in the (then-) Impact Forum in the School of Social Science and Public Policy at King's College London, and to the King's Business School, as well as REF working groups and to a BISA International Law and Politics Working Group workshop, where Mark Reed and Steven Hill also spoke, open to anyone who cared to attend.[1] By that stage, we had identified a further 29 sets of completely 4* ICSs, bringing the total to 111,[2] and continued the investigation to look for anomalies or additional features of note. However, the same characteristics initially identified were found consistently and generally, throughout the review of all ICSs, as we demonstrate in the following analysis.

---

1 We — especially the older one — are grateful, again, to Steven Hill, who kindly also read and commented on the initial draft paper, before the subsequent interim paper was shown and presented to others, and also to Mark Reed, who read the interim paper and offered his thoughts.

2 See Annex 1.

1. Long-term research and impact context

Each of the ICSs reflected a long-term programme of research and a context for impact development. While the research-transformation nexus was important, it was evident that this was rarely a single 'moment' or activity that defined the ICS. For example, Queen Mary University of London's (QMUL) *Promoting Hispanic Performance Cultures* (UoA 35 — Music, Drama, Dance and Performing Arts) relied on numerous and sustained engagement activities with a range of different actors in order to promote, and shift perceptions of, Hispanic performance culture. Similarly, Southampton's *The Music of Michael Finnissy* (UoA 35 — Music, Drama, Dance and Performing Arts) drew on compositions spanning a 40-year period and a range of composition and activity over that period. *Reconfigurable Computing for High-Performance Applications* dated research over 20–30 years to the 1980s (Imperial College London UoA 13 — Electrical Engineering). Of course, 'long term' need not, and rarely would, mean a period of three or four decades — all the more so, because 15 years was the maximum period in which underpinning research could have been published (or, in exceptional situations, 20 years, if a sub-panel had decided to open an extended period in its domain).[3]

Thus, for an impact frame starting in January 2008 (and running to 31 July 2013), the earliest date for research publications was January 1993. That makes it unsurprising that research references might mention the 1990s. For example, 1993 is the first date given for research in the University of East London's (UEL) study on improving psychological understanding of the effects of cigarette and e-cigarette smoking on mood and cognition (*Informing public and policy debate about and improving understanding of the effects of cigarette and e-cigarette smoking*, UEL UoA 4 — Psychology, Psychiatry and Neurology). That research continued over time and involved different researchers at the start to those in the later stages, who were involved, in the main, in delivering impacts. These included the relative benefit of e-cigarettes in alleviating cravings and withdrawal symptoms in abstinent smokers, amelioration of mood issues and alleviating memory impairment — perhaps the most unexpected difference. Of course, this was a relative question — it was not part of the research to cover the serious issues still linked to e-cigarettes, in

---

3 HEFCE, SFC, HEFCW and Department for Employment and Learning NI, *Decisions on assessing research impact* REF 01/11, March 2011, para. 11 (d).

terms of nicotine addiction and the associated health risks (which we would be remiss not to note). All of the relative benefits identified by the researchers for consumers were also used by e-cigarette manufacturers in marketing and in engagement with policy makers, as well as by legislators in passing laws and by the National Health Service and non-governmental organisations (such as ASH — Action on Smoking and Health), in information campaigns. Stretching from research started in 1993, the final impact reported in the study was in June 2013, just a month before the cut-off point for submissions.

Other examples revealing the long-term characteristics include Warwick's study on the reduction of lameness in sheep (*Rapid Antibiotic Treatment Reduces the Prevalence of Lameness caused by Footrot in Sheep*, UoA 6 — Agriculture, Veterinary and Food Science), Bristol's research on the use of aspirin and high dietary fibre in reducing bowel and other cancers (*Use of aspirin and high dietary fibre to prevent and reduce deaths from bowel and other cancers, influencing global policy on cancer prevention and major public health campaigns ('five-a-day')* UoA 1 — Clinical Medicine), and Cardiff's engineering work on engineered barriers to improve nuclear safety and on numerical models more accurately to predict flood risk (*Engineering Solutions for High Level Nuclear Waste Disposal*, UoA 14 — Civil and Construction Engineering), which began in 1999, 1993, 1993 and 1997, respectively. Bristol's contribution to British government policy on private-sector delivery of public services began in the early 1990s (*Affecting private delivery of public services for households and businesses across the UK* UoA 18 — Economics and Econometrics). However, the way in which this work on the effects of policies and 'events' (such as economic shocks) on the risk and cost of capital of private utility companies, shaping regulation of these businesses, affected 'materially … almost every individual and organisation in the UK', did not emerge until 2008 and after. Kingston University's transformation of Historic Royal Palaces (*Cultural and economic impact on Hampton Court Palace from research- based visitor experience* UoA 29 — English) dated its first research from 1999, while most of its research — as with a wide range of other ICSs — stemmed from the early 2000s, around a decade before the REF2014 evaluation. All of these examples confirm the long-term character of research impact found in world-leading studies.

2. Quality/significant research funding

4* ICSs showed evidence of significant, external research funding, with very few exceptions (of which examples are discussed below). Much of the time, this was 'quality' funding from 'premium' funding sources — UK Research Councils (Arts and Humanities Research Board — AHRB, which later became the Arts and Humanities Research Council — AHRC, Economic and Social Research Council — ESRC, the Medical Research Council, Engineering and Physical Sciences Research Council, National Environmental Research Council and so forth) and the Leverhulme Trust. The point can be introduced — and, effectively, summarised — in the name of one Warwick researcher: Wyn Grant! There is a strong correlation between winning grants and conducting research of a type and calibre that might well translate into some wider social, economic, cultural or other human benefit. Curiously, Grant himself was in the Department of Politics and International Studies at Warwick, making him the only researcher from Politics and International Studies known certainly to be involved in a 4* case study (although, surely, some of the studies from Oxford and other places discussed in Chapter 3 must have achieved that level — but with no way of being certain which of them). He contributed to research submitted under agriculture (and including two experts in pesticides and Integrated Pest Management, Dr. David Chandler and Professor Mark Tatchell). In that particular ICS, the research focused on biopesticides, in contrast to synthetic ones, and facilitated the introduction of new regulatory frameworks in the UK for biopesticides and contributed to a 430 per cent rise in their use in the country. That research and impact were the product of research funding from Research Councils UK's RELU programme, the UK government Department for Environment, Farming and Rural Affairs, the European Parliament and the Horticultural Development Company. This exemplified the manner in which a cluster of funding frequently featured in our sample of world-leading ICSs.

Another example, as with so many others, demonstrating a suite of significant research funding is *Improving evidence-based policy and programming for AIDS-affected children in Sub-Saharan Africa.* (Oxford, UoA 22 — Social Work and Social Policy). This research resulted impressively in new policies on psychosocial support and on young carers for parents with AIDS, as well as for orphans, and also the prevention of child-abuse in families affected by the condition, having been embraced by bodies such as UNICEF, Save the Children and USAID (the US government's development agency). The research was underpinned by several projects, with funders including: the ESRC and, jointly, the ESRC and the South African National Research Foundation; the Nuffield Foundation; the South African National Department of Social Development; and the Claude Leon Foundation. In another example, the London School of Economics and Political Science's (LSE) *Better measures of fuel poverty*, which led to a new framework for future action in this area, was enabled by funding of £2.7 million for a Research Centre on Social Exclusion. The presence of funding of this kind was a ready marker that research passed the threshold of being 'internationally excellent' to be considered as underpinning impact — after all, one director of the ESRC, Ian Diamond, had frequently stated that the research councils only funded 'world-leading' research. It was little surprise that such funding featured in world-leading impact case studies.

There was also often significant funding from other important public bodies — government departments, or agencies, the European Commission (EC), the Arts Council, the British Council, cultural organisations and associations. For example, *Stories of a Different Kind: stimulating and shaping new approaches to the representation of disabled people and disability history, arts and culture* (Leicester, UoA 36 — Communication, Cultural and Media Studies) had funding from the National Endowment for Science and Technology, the Heritage Lottery Fund and the Wellcome Trust, as well as the AHRB/AHRC. In the case of Cardiff's civil engineering and construction work on material for better nuclear safety, research was funded by the European Atomic Agency, EURATOM (*Engineering Solutions for High Level Nuclear Waste Disposal*, Cardiff UoA 14 — Civil and Construction Engineering). The UK government's Department for Work and Pensions (DWP) funded research conducted by York University that changed policy and improved service in DWP's JobCentre Plus provision, which included changing use of language in ways that meant discussions about steps towards re-entering the world of work opened up, rather than being closed down (the difference between a focus 'in the future' and 'at the moment', respectively) (*Advising the advisers: improving the conduct of adviser-claimant interviews in JobCentre Plus*, York, UoA 23 — Sociology). These instances indicate the value of research funded by those with a specific interest in the findings.

Some of the ICSs had no evidence of funding from 'premium' sources, but had evidence of significant funding from other sources. These included commissions, as was the case with *The Music of Michael Finnissy* (Southampton, UoA 35 — Music, Drama, Dance and Performing Arts), and the outstanding RNCM's (Royal Northern College of Music) *RNCM's impact on the world-wide development and expansion of the repertoire base and musical practices of professional and amateur symphonic wind orchestras* (UoA 35 — Music, Drama, Dance and Performing Arts). A slightly unusual source of funding for research, though linked to the purpose of the research and its impact, came from Cambridge English

Language Assessment for work by the Centre for Research in English Language Learning and Assessment at the University of Bedfordshire (UoA 29 — English). That research, of which the impact affected millions of individuals, was to improve the validity, dependability and detail of levels and proficiency in tests in English language learning, so the funding was directly relevant, provided by an organisation with a vested interest in a more robust and more reliable testing regime.

As indicated above, in a handful of cases there was no direct reference to research funding. However, in these cases, there can be little doubt that there must have been funding involved. They included *Child Protection: improving practice*, which examined errors in child protection systems and led to an invitation from the UK Secretary of State for Education to review and recommend changes that were adopted (and also picked up in Australia), improving practice in child protection. This research into complex systems would be unlikely — if not impossible — without funding support (although it is possible this was internally generated at the LSE) (LSE, UoA 22 — Social Work). They also included several studies in electrical engineering from Imperial College London, where perhaps there had been a conscious decision, or an assumption, not to mention research funding: case 5 (as numbered by Imperial), which made 'pivotal contributions in the design of power transmission networks, the equipment within these networks, and non-conventional electricity systems' — inter alia, this work fascinatingly showed major over-investment in offshore power, given lower redundancy and security value, as well as the absence of demand offshore itself; case 4, on the transformation of High-Performance Computing and Embedded Design for major transnational businesses; case 3, using ultra-low-power electronics rapidly to diagnose, monitor and treat diseases with confidence, crucially, at low cost; and case 1, *Efficient and Economical Plant Management via Model Predictive Control*, used by a range of industries and multinational companies (Imperial College London, UoA 13 — Electrical Engineering). Curiously, the remaining study submitted by Imperial did include reference to funding, suggesting that the absence of mentions otherwise was not a question of institutional approach. The other Imperial cases might have been because the authors had decided consciously not to mention funding, or because it had not occurred to them to do so, which, as also with the possibility of a university's policy, could explain the absence of references to funding where, in practice, it could be expected that the research would not have been possible without it.

Two of the 111 case studies examined in this research may not have had any external funding input, even implicitly — even if it is conceivable that there was 'invisible' funding in each of them. The first of these was Kingston University's contribution to the 'Hacked Off' campaign, which Professor Brian Cathcart co-founded, and, subsequently, to the Leveson Inquiry in the UK into newspaper hacking of private phones and the eventual passage of legislation through Parliament and a new Royal Charter on press regulation, in which Cathcart and colleagues played leading roles (Kingston University, *Impact on the Leveson Inquiry and press regulation in the UK*, UoA 29 — English Language and Literature). The second was one of the most singular and interesting studies, Newcastle's *Red Dust Road*, which is based around the literary creativity of writer Jackie Kay, who became a professor in the Newcastle Centre for Literary Arts (NCLA) (Newcastle, UoA 29 — English). The only indication of potential funding concerns the Northern Arts Fellowship that originally took Kay to the university — as the Arts Council of England backs the Fellowship, it must be presumed that there is funding associated with it, but neither the Arts Council, nor the NCLA offers much information at all on it (renamed the North Eastern Literary Fellowship), including no information on funding. The only clear reference to funding — and the only reference to funding directly at the time of research and impact — concerns support from the university itself for a PhD student to undertake research trips with Kay to her 'ancestral' village. However, remarkably, there was no other indication of funding for the 'brilliant' research activity itself (the word that writer and broadcaster Mariella Frostrup is quoted using in the ICS) and the equally brilliant impact regarding adoption and race — evidenced in book sales, educational impact, public discourse, life enhancement and individuals ('made me feel more understood and seen'). Thus, while overwhelmingly and generally, top-level impact case studies explicitly show evidence of external funding, and otherwise, funding is implicit, *Red Dust Road* is an exception that shows that, although rare, top-level research and impact can be achieved, in principle, without such funding.

3. Clear engagement/an embedded role in implementation/researcher-practitioner unity

A common feature in our analysis is the role played by researchers in translating the research into impact. Researchers might be invited to play a contributing role, or they might play a leading role in translating research into a transformative difference, and, indeed, they might be researcher-practitioners, i.e., researchers who also engage in practice and so directly translate research into impact. These include: curatorial or advisory roles, such as Southampton's *At Home with Music* (UoA 35 — Music, Drama, Dance and Performing Arts) and Leicester's *Stories of a different kind* (UoA 36 — Communication, Cultural and Media Studies). They also involved researcher-practice, for instance, QMUL's *Transforming Publics and Participation through Performance*, in which Lois Weaver, singled-handed, combined the roles of researcher, artist, curator and activist to affect the practice of emerging and established artists and performance planning and curation, as well as bringing 'citizens' from often excluded and marginal backgrounds 'to contribute meaningfully to discussions of urgent social issues, including human rights, sexuality, aging [sic] and new technologies' (UoA 35 — Music, Drama, Dance and Performing Arts). These case studies in the realm of the arts and communication focused the role of the individual in implementing impact in perhaps more alternative frames.

More often and more conventionally, engagement and embedding involved the worlds of policy, practice and commerce. For example, two studies already mentioned involved full engagement between researcher and impact: York's study, *Advising the advisers: improving the conduct of adviser-claimant interviews in JobCentre Plus*, which was embedded with JobCentre Plus and the DWP, including a stream of policy papers internally for the Department; and *Impact on the Leveson Inquiry and press regulation in the UK*, from Kingston, where Brian Cathcart led Hacked Off's interventions with government, drafting a Royal Charter and amendments to it, as well as advising the House of Commons Culture, Media and Sport Select Committee. Another study on developing higher education in further education saw HEFCE funding advice and assistance from the University of Sheffield on developing policy, as well as engaging with the Department for Business, Innovation and Skills, providing consultancy to the Learning and Skills Improvement Service, and serving as members of the Association of Colleges, the Higher Education Academy and the Quality Assurance Agency for Higher Education (Sheffield, UoA 25 — Education). Internationally, Gareth Stansfield's research at Exeter led to his being appointed as Senior Political Advisor to the United Nations (UN) Secretary-General's Special Representative in Iraq, in which role he engaged with Kurdish political leaders on strategy, on behalf of the Special Representative. Subsequently, his work led to the drafting of recommendations on the resolution of disputed territories around Kirkuk for the UN Department of Political Affairs. That shaped the UN Assistance Mission in Iraq report on disputed boundaries in Iraq (*Political Dynamics in post-2003 Iraq*, Exeter, UoA 27 — Area Studies).

In the commercial domain, research at Swansea on *The development of food items to benefit cognition and mood*, already mentioned in terms of its long-term development, made significant differences. As well as having major impact on policy with the European Food Information Council and the US Department of Agriculture and Food, work led by David Benton also benefited commercial food production and marketing, with major companies, such as Kraft and Danône. Research showing the positive effects on children's memory and cognition of slow-release sugars (such as those from wholemeal products — this later became received knowledge) had been picked up, and funded and supported by Danône, in France, which developed its 'Petit Dejeuner Lu', later sold on to Kraft outside France and re-branded BelVita around the world and in France, generating £50 million in sales, in 2013. The product was said to have 'revolutionised' the biscuit market, with marketing focused around 'the beneficial effect on cognitive functioning.' Benton's research at Swansea and individual leadership played a 'critical' role in complex commercial processes (Swansea, UoA 4 — Psychology, Psychiatry and Neurology).

More conventional and policy-oriented instances, involving contributions to report writing and to embedded policy implementation, were the LSE's *Citizens Interests* (UoA 36 — Communication, Cultural and Media Studies) and, epitomising this aspect of impact, *Empowering Children Online* (UoA 36 — Communication, Cultural and Media Studies). In the latter, Sonia Livingstone developed transformative research regarding the need to facilitate online access for the poorest children and the educational and other benefits this would bring, but also the need for and means to provide online protection of children, which, in turn, could be seen to have empowered children. Livingstone's research not only directly informed the Byron Review which adopted a model developed in her research and the UK Department of Education's Home Access Programme but she herself was involved in embedded implementation. She served on the Home Secretary's Task Force for Child Protection on the Internet and on the Department of Education's Home Access Programme and an associated panel, as well as being commissioned by OFCOM (the Office of Communications — the UK communications regulator) to provide its evidence to the Byron Review, and also being appointed as Evidence Champion, Board Member and founding Evidence Group Chair to the UK Council for Child Internet Safety, itself a body created partly as a result of her research. This role in embedded implementation was echoed internationally, as she led the EU Kids Online network, which informed, advised and shaped policy in national and European Union (EU) contexts, as well as other international bodies, such as UNICEF, the

International Telecommunication Union and the Organisation for Economic Co-operation and Development (OECD), as well as presenting the research, inter alia, to the EC's Safer Internet Forum, European Commission, European Parliament, Swedish Presidency of the EU, and Insafe, Internet Governance Forum, Family Online Safety Institute. Livingstone's study offered an exemplary version of an individual's commitment and engagement in delivering impact, and, indeed, was one of the most impressive.

4. Resource/financial commitment to impact

The 4* ICSs included evidence of a clear commitment of resources by the beneficiaries — an indication of the benefit and their welcome for the research. Investment in translating research into impact could be financial, or the commitment of resources, or the generation of further money and resources. For example, Colonial Williamsburg Foundation paid for the 'Threads of Feelings' exhibition to travel to the US (University of Hertfordshire, *Threads of Feeling* — UoA 30, History). This was the kind of commitment of resources — the money to transport across the Atlantic (both ways) and to cover insurance, the costs of installing and exhibiting — that suggested just how significant the research and its output had been. This was supplemented by 'impact' funding from AHRC — surely a signal of impact quality. It was further augmented by other aspects, such as sales of books, a re-created printed textile, CDs of period songs (selected by John Styles, the lead researcher) and entries to the exhibition — 15,000 visitors paid to see the commercial version of the exhibition at Olympia in London, while 46,619 at the DeWitt Wallace Decorative Arts Museum in Virginia. This is a rich example of the variety of resources, financial and other commitments that can mark out and confirm impact.

The commitment of resources to expanding and exploiting research ranges across similar examples. *Empowering Children Online though Literacy and safe Initiatives* sparked the UK government to commit resources to found and establish the UK Council for Child Internet Safety and the creation of its *Child Internet Safety Strategy*, as well as the Department of Education's commitment to offer reduced-cost, safe computer and internet access for the UK's poorest children, while prompting resource commitments by international bodies, including the EU, the OECD and UNICEF (LSE — UoA 36). *Accountability and Victims' Rights in Peace Processes* offered further instances of investment, broadly understood. Based on research by the Transitional Justice Institute at the University of Ulster, this was an ICS framed around benefits to various stakeholders of research on peace processes and human rights. The Basque Government committed major resources to peace steps in its own region, while in the Philippines, major peacebuilding non-governmental actors — such as Conciliation Resources and International Alert — and the Norwegian Government did likewise (University of Ulster UoA 20 — Law). Another case study from the same stable, which involved both artist and community participation, attracted resources both at grassroots level in Northern Ireland with the Bridge of Hope, the Ashton Community Trust and the Community Relations Council, and from the American development agency, USAID (*Framing Transitional Justice Practice: Dealing with the Past in Northern Ireland*, University of Ulster, UoA 20 — Law).

Sales constituted a manifestation of resource generation — both in commercially oriented ICSs, such as Psychology at Swansea's *The development of food items to benefit cognition and mood* (discussed above) and culturally oriented studies in English and Modern Languages — again, Newcastle's *Red Dust Road*, with extensive sales, was discussed above, in English. Other studies in the English category also showed benefit in sales. These included Kingston's work developing creative writing with military veterans as a form of coping with post-combat stress, which generated profits that contributed to aiding 50,000 people via the Soldiers, Sailors and Airmen Family Association (though this was not the main benefit of the research, even, as that lay in the catharsis of creative writing — *The Military Writing Network: Creative Writing, Life Writing and Trauma* Kingston UoA 29 — English). In the same UoA, they also involved Swansea's *Father knows Lloyd George. Now so do thousands of others: expanding theatre audiences and enriching history in post-devolution Wales* and the remarkable research contribution to The Library of Wales: *Influencing Government Policy to benefit the Creative Industries, Cultural Tourism, Education and General Readers*, a collection of neglected English-language Welsh literature, which sold 56,000 copies and gave new life to a small Welsh publisher, among other mainly cultural and policy impacts (Swansea, UoA 29 — English). But, in many respects, the smaller volume of sales for Cardiff's translation and transformation of the high points of Welsh literature (largely unknown, given the relatively small numbers of Welsh speakers), the medieval collection of tales, *The Mabinogion*, which sold over 32,000 copies, was more impressive (*Transforming the Mabinogion*, UoA 28 — Modern Languages). Sales, such as these, showed the difference research in some domains could make.

One of UCL's (University College London) criminology studies brought investment from the UK Home Office and various British police forces, as well as in Edmonton, Canada, (*Improving police practice and reducing the incidence of crime through mapping and analysis*, UCL, UoA 22 — Social Work and Social Policy), while another did the same and also gained major support from New Zealand Police and the US Department of Justice (*Situational crime prevention policy and practice*, UCL, UoA 22 — Social Work and Social Policy). Each of them resulted in major crime reduction. The latter did so through an understanding of context — the situational detail that could affect the commission of crimes — the design of bicycle racks could impede theft of bicycles, while understanding the social networks and processes used by criminals in domestic child sexual exploitation could result in disruption of them and, so, reduction in the incidence of the crimes involved. The former could predict the spread of burglaries by neighbourhood spread (the UCL original research), and, following development involving researchers at UCLA (the University of California Los Angeles) in a time-stable manner (the UCLA input). This led to prevention. Burglaries predicted were burglaries that could be prevented — and were, with up to 66 per cent prevented, where the UCL mapping approach was applied. The former also included another aspect of further resource development — a spin-out company, which, in this instance, was based in the US, and followed the UCL researchers' being invited to present their work at UCLA, where commercially available predictive mapping software was developed, adding commercial revenue and job-creation impact to that of crime reduction.

Spin-out, or spin-off, companies were a fairly common feature of impact case studies in fields such as medicine and allied areas, and applied science — often also entailing job creation and sales, given the commercial intention in forming a spin-out company. Electrical Engineering at Imperial College London reported nine spin-out companies created, two of which were in the focused study of the next-generation semi-conductor sequencing — replacing the process of using fluorescent tagging of target DNA which will then latch onto, and so identify, matching DNA (but is slower and reliant on optical methods of identification), this process of label-free (i.e. without tagging) electrochemical DNA detection uses an ion-sensitive field effect transistor to provide a low-cost and high-benefit detection, monitoring and treatment of diseases (*Case 3 — Ultra-Low-Power Electronics for Healthcare Applications*, Imperial College London, UoA 13 — Electrical Engineering). In Medicine and its allied fields, such as Healthcare and Pharmacy, spin-out companies were so frequent in impact case studies that it was a striking moment when an ICS explicitly mentioned the 'improved clinical outcomes' of pharmaceutical research that gave a step-change benefit to HIV and Hepatitis C sufferers (as well as enormous profits to Janssen, the company manufacturing and marketing the improved formulation drugs, as well as delivering not-for-profit supplies to 'resource-limited countries') (*Supporting regulatory approval of poorly soluble drugs for HIV and Hepatitis C*, Nottingham, UoA 3 — Pharmacy). Of course, in fairness, benefits to patients were mentioned, or implicit, in the creation of spin-out companies in the wide range of ICSs where they occurred. For example, Dundee's *Biomedical informatics transforming the care of people with chronic diseases internationally* related improved patient care and health treatment — reducing both amputations and sight-threatening retinopathy linked to diabetes by 40 per cent, as well as the creation of a new business that attracted over £10 million investment (and also government policy) (Dundee, UoA 1 — Clinical Medicine). However, some studies left the clinical benefit more implicit — two Bristol studies mentioned clinical trials, but did not mention the clinical outcome (respectively, *Translating research into novel immunotherapies delivers scientific and economic gains for the pharmaceutical/biotechnology sector in drug discovery*, and *New businesses, commercial investment and adoption of new technology result from antigen-specific peptide immunotherapy development*, Bristol, UoA 1 — Clinical Medicine). That focus on the business investment aspect underlined the significance of attracting and generating resources as a measure of impact.

5. Quotes as evidence and presentation

With one exception, all 4* ICSs in our initial study used direct quotation as evidence of impact achieved; the one that did not used close reference that might have been presented as quotation (and we would suggest should have). In the span of 111 cases analysed, this remained the general trend — most 4* ICSs including direct quotation and those that did not using a form of close reference that should, really, have been as direct quotation for clearer and stronger effect. An example of close reference, in this context, can be seen in *Changing Policy And Practice in the Prevention of Suicide And Self-Harm*, which points out that the research by Stirling is 'cited' in guidelines by both the National Institute for Health and Care Excellence and the Royal College of Psychiatrists (UoA 4 — Psychology). While this shows the strength of the case, it is possible that clear, direct quotation might have given the case even greater strength.

Certainly, in some instances, marking the best ones, the ICS impact section featured extensive quotation and, sometimes, could seem

almost entirely made of quotations demonstrating the impact, such as
The Old Bailey Online (Hertfordshire — UoA 30, History). Paragraphs
were packed with supporting quotation, as this small extract from one
of them illustrates:

> In 2012 David Willetts, then minister for Universities and Science,
> said the website 'provided a valuable resource' to academics and
> researchers, and was also 'source material for creative industries'.
> [Ref. 6] Old Bailey Online material formed the basis of BBC1's
> hugely successful Garrow's Law, which ran for three series between
> 2009 and 2011, winning the Royal Television Society Award for
> best drama. Series creator Tony Marchant said in 2009 that his
> interest arose 'after the Old Bailey had published online transcripts
> of cases going back 200 years. These transcripts were a fantastic
> oral and written account of the period ... the words of the accused
> and the prosecutors gave me an insight into the history.' [Ref. 7]

Other examples packed with nicely used quotation include *Changing
policy on competition in the UK health-care market to benefit patients
and taxpayers* (Bristol, UoA 18 — Economics), an extreme example, at
times almost all quotation from officials in the Department of Health.
A similarly extreme example, at times almost entirely rendered with
quotation, is Swansea's study, *Father knows Lloyd George. Now so do
thousands of others: expanding theatre audiences and enriching history
in post-devolution Wales* (Swansea, UoA 29 — English). Elsewhere,
both of Sheffield's ICSs in the Education rubric made full use of
quotation, as well — especially *Raising Early Achievement in Literacy*,
which has some paragraphs rippling with strong quotation (Sheffield,
UoA 25 — Education). These ICSs revealed the advantages of rich use
of quotation in presenting impact.

Promoting Hispanic Performance Cultures (QMUL, UoA 35 —
Music, Drama, Dance and Performing Arts) also offered a particularly
strong and striking example of using quotations, actually using them
to *frame* Section 4. The section detailing impact, as a whole, opens
with a quotation and each of the subsequent three sections identifying
discrete areas of impact does the same — as can be seen in the example
here, showing the opening of that section:

4. Details of Impact

*Professor Delgado has perhaps more than anyone in recent years had
a profound influence on the perceptions of people in Britain on*

Spanish theatre. She has widened our perspective and deepened our knowledge of Spanish writers, playwrights, directors and theatre practice. — Sir Brian McMaster, Advisor to the Cultural Olympiad (2012), author of 'McMaster Review: Supporting excellence in the arts — from measurement to judgement' (DCMS, 2008), former Director of the Edinburgh International Festival (1992–2006)

Delgado's research in theatrical and screen cultures has generated a body of knowledge that has led to impact in three key areas.

I. Opening up public discourse

I've always appreciated María's insight regarding theatre matters, and especially her advice to me during my time as Director of the Grec Festival in Barcelona [2006–11]. Her reviews, comments and perceptions about the international scene resulted in my inviting many highly appreciated artists to present their work in our programmes. — Ricardo Szwarcer, Director of Usina del Arte, Buenos Aires (2012)

Delgado has made 30+ BBC radio appearances to discuss Spanish and Latin-American stage and screen culture across six different programmes: ... [Bold and italic use as in the original]

Structuring the ICS around these quotations is highly effective, giving the reader strong evidence, even before they have read further detail — but, when analysis follows the quotation, it seamlessly combines to leave little doubt of the quality.

Another approach to using quotes, adopted in a different submission to the same UoA by Queen Mary, was to use a set of them to open the details section with direct evidence — while, in contrast, a study from Goldsmiths, also in that same category, had a series of strong quotes in its final paragraph. These are both reproduced at length to show the effect of this dense use of quotation. The first of them is *Cultural Policy and Practice Exchanges between Britain and Brazil* (QMUL, UoA 35 — Music, Drama, Dance and Performing Arts):

4. Details of the impact ...

Heritage's work brings culture to the centre of the agenda ... Heritage is well known across Brazil as intellectual, teacher, researcher, international mediator and creative artist, whose engagement to the nation's social development ... is recognised by his wide circle of interlocutors with admiration, solidarity and gratitude. — L. E. Soares, former National Secretary of Public Security, Ministry of Justice [see www.peoplespalace.org.uk].

In his stagings of Shakespeare in slum areas in the middle of tremendous violence where different groups of heavily armed drug traffickers confronted each other on a daily basis, art brought peace to the region. It was enough for many to realize that it was a concrete possibility worth fighting for. — Julita Lemgruber, Director of Rio's Centre for Studies in Public Security and Citizenship [CESeC], University Candido Mendes, May 2013 [see www.peoplespalace.org.uk].

I and other senior colleagues have been actively engaged in debate, in reading your papers, in exchange with this programme [Points of Contact] that aims to increase the capacity of artists, policy makers and funders to realise the full potential of dynamic and transformative cultural actions. Partly as a result of this engagement, we designed and launched a new 10 year programme, Creative People and Places which seeks to engage communities in the UK in new and radically different approaches to develop inspiring and sustainable arts programmes. — Moira Sinclair, ACE Executive Director London and the South East [see section 5]

Heritage's research seeks contemporary purpose in creative practices, and insists that social justice, development and enterprise are only possible through the inclusion of those who are behind the '*doors on the peripheries*' (Soares). His influence on new thinking in cultural policy and new forms of artistic practice is evidenced through inter-connected research projects.

The example of packing quotation at the end is *Supporting Afghan music in the post-Taliban era* (Goldsmiths, UoA 35 — Music, Drama, Dance and Performing Arts):

Public affirmation

Abdul Wahab Madadi, a renowned Afghan singer and writer, and the former Head of Music of Afghan Radio and Television, spoke at Baily and Doubleday's Now Ruz concert for the Afghan community in Hamburg (14 March 2008).[7] He asserted that:

"[their] contribution to awareness of Afghan music has been much greater than anything the Afghanistan Ministry of Culture has done towards [sic] our culture and heritage".

The Noor TV broadcast of the (aforementioned) Goldsmiths concert ended with viewers phoning in with their comments.[8] Viewers thanked Noor TV for broadcasting *"one of the best music groups"*, who *"play the real Afghan music"*. One viewer said:

"I have known John Baily and Veronica Doubleday for a long time and they are people who are in love with Afghan music, culture and heritage. We must support them for keeping true Afghan music alive."

Baily and Doubleday's work has been praised at length in Nasruddin Saljoqi's Persian translation and adaptation of Baily's CUP monograph *Music of Afghanistan: Professional musicians in the city of Herat* (1988), published in Kabul in 2010.[9]

On 10 November 2012 Baily and Doubleday were honoured by the Herati community in London, when they gave a concert in The Music Room, an Afghan venue in Wembley. Among speeches by Afghans praising their work was the statement by Dr Hamid Simab, a retired psychiatrist and social activist living in Canada:

"Afghanistan for the last 35 years has been devastated in all aspects: political, social, economic, spiritual. But nowhere is this devastation more keenly felt than in the realm of artistic expression … all of us, as Afghans who have inherited what remains of our cultural heritage, are so deeply indebted to [Baily and Doubleday] for their lives' work … from the bottom of my heart — as an Afghan who appreciates your work, and I can say, on behalf of all Afghans — thank you for what you have done for us, thank you for what you have done for the culture of our country."[10]

In August 2011 Baily received an Illuminated Address from the Ministry of Information and Culture office in Herat: *"Your valuable and tireless service in the strengthening and growth of the Herat music abroad is truly appreciated."*[11]

Whether densely packed at the opening, to set the keynote for the impact to be shown, or richly displayed at the end, as a final flurry of fireworks, as these full examples show, the effect can be overwhelming.

As with structuring the whole impact section around quotation, the key is use of quotation — especially when it is so extensive and used so judiciously, as in the examples shown here. Overall, the presence of quotation — or, even, close reference — was a strong indicator of the high-calibre impact being described. The more extensive the quotation, the stronger the sense of impact — and the more skilfully that quotation was used structurally to give emphasis in the presentation, the more immediately convincing and intense was the sense of world-leading impact.

In the course of this chapter, we have shown through close analysis of case studies, the first five of eight characteristics of world-leading impact. These are long-term research and impact context; the presence of research funding, especially from significant or 'premium' sources; evidence of clear engagement, or an embedded role in implementation; notable resource, or financial commitment to impact; and the use of direct quotes (and, if not, close reference, where quotes should have been used), both as evidence and to assist in presentation and structure. In Chapter 7, we shall develop analysis of the remaining three characteristics: 6. the density of case studies, demonstrating combinations of breadth and range, with a rich multiplicity of smaller and larger differences made, all generating a cumulative effect; 7. the seemingly unavoidable hallmark of any impact — creating something new, or offering something transformative for beneficiaries; and 8. finally, and, to some extent, controversially, news media and public engagement.

7 The eight characteristics of world-leading, 4* impact: 6–8

In Chapter 6, we outlined the first five of the eight characteristics common to 4* impact case studies (ICSs) in the Research Excellence Framework REF2014, identified through our close-reading analysis. In the present chapter, we develop the three outstanding qualities, in three sections: 6. breadth/range/multiplicity/cumulative effect; 7. creating something new/transformative for beneficiaries; and 8. news media engagement and public engagement. Having set out and exemplified each of the characteristics, we conclude with consolidation of our typology, alongside consideration of caveats and the issue of exceptions, including one, in a particularly exceptional study, which, while sharing the essential characteristic of all research impact, making a big difference, lacked evidence of most of the other qualities we identified more generally.

6. Breadth/range/multiplicity/cumulative effect

It is striking that 4* ICSs generally have a range of impacts, suggesting a cumulative effect and continuing radial waves of impact. According to Mark Reed's Fast Track Impact research, the average number of 'impacts' per high-scoring case study in 2014 was 2.8.[1] This is an indication that impact is rarely one single or simple outcome. That means that it should be expected that ICSs would have a compound character, involving multiple and a potentially broad range of effects, which add up to the whole. However, while this reflects our concern in this section, in part, it does not do so wholly. As we shall see, there are some studies

---

1 Mark Reed et al., 'Steps to a top-scoring impact case study', *Comment Nature Index*, 12 July 2018 available at www.natureindex.com/news-blog/steps-to-a-top-scoring-impact-case-study at 21 December 2019.

where scope and reach are indicated not in two or three major steps, but in something more like a cascade of smaller features.

Impact had various aspects and features and demonstrating them was perhaps important in indicating scope and reach. In some instances, this could mean taking one development and showing how different users adopted it. *Case 1 — Efficient and Economical Plant Management via Model Predictive Control* (Imperial College London, UoA 13 — Electrical Engineering) explained how research on linear and non-linear model predictive control had been exploited by major businesses. Honeywell had adopted the model in advance control technology and used it in three areas of their activity: first, for ethylene production by the largest producer of polypropylene in the world, German company Basell Polyolefins GmBH; secondly, for use in power plants, for China's Sinopec; and, thirdly, they created a whole new business division of their own around the research for automotive powertrains. Swiss-Swedish ABB used the same model in cement manufacture and, as with Honeywell and Sinopec, in power plants. In a similar way, Dundee's *Biomedical informatics transforming the care of people with chronic diseases internationally* (Dundee, UoA 1 — Medicine) had a string of different forms of impact: on health outcomes in Scotland, through National Health Service (NHS) Scotland practice; on Scottish government policy; on commercial development through business and job creation; and on Kuwait, where Dundee's health informatics platform was introduced via a joint Scotland-Kuwait initiative that also benefited the Scottish side financially, initially worth £15 million. Another example of one piece of research having repeated and expanded impact is *The impact of alcohol test purchasing by underage adolescents on the availability of alcohol to minors* (Swansea, UoA 4 — Psychology, Psychiatry and Neurology). Pilot research showed the scale on which, even where ID had been checked, alcohol was still sold to minors, and this research allowed police and, even more, local trading standards officials, to take action to reduce the availability. As a result of legal changes, every police force and local authority trading standards department in England and Wales adopted alcohol test purchasing to enforce the law — resulting in significant reductions in underage alcohol purchasing and, because of this, consumption reduced by 60 per cent in Thames Valley and West Yorkshire police areas, according to the research. Reviewing these cases, the compound nature of examples such as these clearly confirms the manifold character of impact. But, through the multiple aspects of these cases, they remain reasonably straightforward.

In other cases, as indicated, the compound character of impact was more complex. The weight, density, accumulation and richness of smaller impacts was a key feature in demonstrating impact and transformation. While one study used the term 'accumulated' to capture its various impacts, this was not even one of the more significantly condensed cases (*Raising Early Achievement in Literacy*, Sheffield, UoA 25 — Education). This study showed how impact was rolled out in smaller stages, first with 60 practitioners and 680 children from 500 families, but extended through work with non-profit organisations and their cooperation with different local authorities across eight projects, to result in 3,800 practitioners being trained, and eventually, 150,000 families. However, the most striking illustrations of dense, compound impact were found in other studies.

For example, RNCM's (Royal Northern College of Music) ICS, *RNCM's impact on the world-wide development and expansion of the repertoire base and musical practices of professional and amateur symphonic wind orchestras* (RNCM, UoA 35 — Music, Drama, Dance and Performing Arts) referenced compositions, to start its case, suggesting that many new pieces had been created, and confirming 25 new compositions for different types and levels of ensemble by Adam Gorb, and that six of these were in the top 35 downloads from the specialist music publisher for this type of work, as well as identifying an international array of bands, from the US Marines to Singapore, that had benefited from playing the new music. The ICS continued with exposition of performances around the world, confirmed by YouTube recordings of them, for example, and also included rippling detail on CD sales, educational activities, public engagement and increasing capacity (by revitalising wind music and providing new material to be performed) to demonstrate impact. The same institution's very different but, perhaps, even more impressive study on a new opera, *Anya 17*, by composer Adam Gorb and librettist Ben Kaye, also revealed the cumulative effect of mushrooming detail of impacts. The opera, on the unexpected topic of sex trafficking, engaged with 11 anti-trafficking organisations, generated public awareness through YouTube and Facebook channels, before being picked up by various politicians, including then-immigration minister Damian Green, and also performed internationally, including in Romania, from where the title character is said to come. This swell of major and minor effects simply removed any possibility of doubt about the value of research impact.

7. Creating something new/transformative for beneficiaries

Given that impact is about making a difference in the real world, it is inevitable that the one sure element in any ICS had to be the sense of a real change. Impact in the 4* studies was clearly transformative, almost always taking something from nothing to something and beyond. While a 20-year career and programme of research might be crucial in setting up the context, and radial waves of cumulative impact might occur, it was creating something novel, in terms of impact, that made the big difference. In this respect, it is notable that research-led creative practice might have a potential advantage over other fields, as research leading to creative outputs that then are extended to users, audiences and communities clearly follows the nothing-creation-something-impact trajectory. In the remainder of the present section, we introduce a selection of case studies that illustrate real changes made by research[2] — and also something of the surprising variety in the realm of research impact, from medicine and health through to poetry and play.

Our first examples all come from the quite stunning submissions from Bristol in Clinical Medicine (UoA 1) and in Public Health (UoA 2). Two of the studies in the first category simply engender the response, 'Wow!' One of them innovated with the pioneering bioengineered trachea and upper bronchus replacement in a 30-year-old woman with acute breathing problems, using her own stem cells and cells from a cadaver trachea. The only alternative would have been a highly risky lung removal, a procedure associated with a high mortality rate. Yet, only four days after the decellularised scaffold trachea was seeded with the recipient's own cells and other cells to replicate the inside lining of the trachea, the woman's upper left bronchus was replaced with the graft and she not only survived, but gained a healthy life, not even needing her immune system to be suppressed, nor continuing healthcare. This inherently awe-inspiring impact was amplified not only in mainstream media, but also became a feature in the 'Who am I?' permanent exhibition at the Science Museum, in London (*Health benefits, increased public awareness and changes in national policy result from the successful implantation of the first tissue-engineered trachea, created utilising the patient's own stem cells*, Bristol, UoA 1 — Clinical Medicine). The other example involved the development of a research-based maternity unit training package that resulted, inter alia, in a 50 per cent reduction in perinatal hypoxia, a

---

2 This selection is, by definition, selective, given that each of the 111 ICSs represented notable differences being made. So, others could have been chosen. The choice here reflects variety and also, inevitably, some of those that represented some of the more surprising aspects of impact.

90 per cent drop in brachial plexus injuries, and — in a quite different type of benefit — a 91 per cent reduction in payouts and litigation costs at the Bristol Southmead hospital, where the researchers first introduced the package, with similar financial outcomes of improved health outcomes identified in pilot schemes in the US and Australia (*Delivering better birthdays: research-based training programme makes labour and birth safer for babies and mothers across the world*, Bristol, UoA 1 — Clinical Medicine).

Moving from Clinical Medicine, the second category of remarkable impact from Bristol is in public health and concerns treatment guidelines for HIV positive people (*Improving treatment guidelines, life expectancy and access to life insurance for HIV positive people*, UoA 2 — Public Health, Health Services and Primary Care). This includes improved treatment and increased life expectancy. These are welcome differences. They are also ones that it could be hoped that researchers in the realms of medicine and public health would be making. That is not to question the value of making this difference — in itself immense and worthy of a world-leading classification. The particularly surprising aspect of this study, however, was the presentation of tremendous enhancement of quality of life, especially in the way insurance companies revolutionised their approach to — and the availability of — products for those with the condition, but receiving the improved treatment. That improvement concerned the timing of Antiretroviral Therapy (ART), which showed convincingly that something called the CD4 count was the key factor in balancing AIDS prevention and longer life, on one hand, and the harmful side effects of the ART. This made the CD4 count the defining point for treatment — with 350 cells/mm the key point. The difference was considerable: a 20 year old starting treatment with <100 cells/mm had life expectancy to 38; a 20 year old starting treatment with 200–350 cells/mm had life expectancy over 53. As a result of the Bristol research, international guidelines were updated to introduce earlier treatment, and policy makers and practitioners promoted earlier treatment, based on the findings. Of course, the principal beneficiaries were the patients themselves — and, as indicated, not only simply in terms of health and length of life, but also quality of life. Just as the research broadly generated public awareness of the deficits of starting treatment late, its knock-on effect on quality of life was remarkable. The research led to changes in the availability of insurance. Several insurance companies based their revised assessments on the Bristol team's published research and others later followed suit. As a consequence, there was 'increased normalisation of HIV compared to other chronic diseases', with life assurance policies becoming available to those taking the ART from the right point — and having a life assurance span of 20 years or more also meant that previously unattainable mortgages became available, as did business loans, transforming life possibilities.

Other health-related cases include two studies contributing notably to suicide prevention policy and practice. As the studies between them show, suicide is a major personal and economic issue, with each successful attempt affecting at least six surviving people seriously, carrying a hefty emotional strain, and costing £1,290,000 (at the time of the Stirling study[3]). One of these involved University of Stirling research in Psychology that meant suicide prevention could be based on evidence for the first time. Situational research identified the mixture of mechanisms and risks that lead individuals to acts of self-harm and to attempt, or to commit, suicide (*Changing Policy And Practice In the Prevention Of Suicide*, Stirling, UoA 4 — Psychology, Psychiatry and Neurology). The research meant that an area of policy and practice that had previously not been able to engender a real difference was now able to do so. The team's Integrated Motivational-Volitional model could look at the 'proximal mechanisms' that could translate risk into reality — such as, notably, 'perfectionism', 'sensitivity to defeat' and 'entrapment (the final pathway to suicide …).' This made it possible to distinguish why one individual suffering depression might be at greater risk of suicide than another with that condition — or, why fewer than five people in a hundred suffering depression are suicidal. This took understanding of self-harm and suicide beyond psychiatric disorder explanations, providing personality and cognitive risk supplements that could explain when 'distal risk' could be translated into suicidal behaviour. As a result, policy, clinical guidelines and practice were changed, whether informing schools on expectation management and including perfectionism in risk-assessment protocols, or local authority and clinical diagnosis, contributing to the reduction of suicide, notably in rural areas.

The second study contributing to suicide prevention also both focused on detail and mechanics, and contributed to policy and practice changes. The study, involving researchers at the University of Bristol,

---

3 In 2016, the average cost was put at £1.7 million per suicide and a minimum of 16 people affected by each suicide 'behaviour.' Terry Rigby, *Suicide and Suicide Prevention: An overview of current challenges and future opportunities*, NP: Forward for Life, 2016.

focused on restricting access to highly lethal methods — one of the most effective strategies for prevention (*Fewer suicides worldwide following changes in policy and practice influenced by University of Bristol research*, Bristol, UoA 2 — Public Health, Health Services and Primary Care). The study indicated that most individuals who survive an attempt to commit suicide, 'even one using a high-lethality method', do not try again. Given this position and also, we might suggest, that suicide might often be impulsive and, where there is a chance for second thought, is questioned, then focusing prevention on the most lethal methods may be the best approach to giving individuals the chance for reflection and continuing life, and avoiding the emotional blows to those close to them. The researchers showed that under 1 per cent of those using paracetamol and other analgesics resulted in death; by contrast, those using a tablespoon of paraquat weedkiller, resulted in death on seven out of ten occasions, and those jumping from high structures had a 95 per cent death rate.[4] Despite the low incidence of suicide completion using paracetamol and anti-depressants, understanding how availability can affect successful use led to interventions resulting in reductions in death. Paracetamol and co-proxamol, between them, accounted for around half of painkiller suicides. The withdrawal of co-proxamol led to 600 fewer suicides using it, while restrictions on paracetamol pack size and the number of packets (two) that could be purchased at a time, was shown by research to have resulted in reduced deaths and liver transplant operations. At the other end of the lethality of means scale, in the researchers' own neighbourhood, the erection of high barriers halved the number of suicide jumps from the Clifton Suspension Bridge (and no evidence of displacement to other sites, so an overall halving of one of the most likely means of completing suicide). This was an approach

4 Other research in the US, where the high availability of firearms adds significantly to the range of high-lethality methods, reported the death rate involving guns as 91 per cent of attempts completed and 51 per cent of all suicides involved guns. That research confirmed that over 90 per cent of those who had made an attempt would ultimately die from other causes; and it also appeared to indicate that those who did make a further attempt that was also not completed were most likely to make repeated attempts, and that more than half of those who made a further attempt that was completed did so within five years of the initial attempt. See Merete Nordentoft, Trine Madsen and Annette Erlangsen, 'You Seldom Get a Second Chance With a Gunshot: Lethality of Suicidal Acts', Editorial, *The American Journal of Psychiatry* Vol. 173 No. 11 2016 available at https://ajp.psychiatryonline.org/doi/full/10.1176/appi.ajp.2016.16080943?af=R at 26 December 2019.

adopted further afield, including at another notorious suicide site, the Archway Bridge in North London, and its being cited in the official strategy document in England.[5] The effect of both the Stirling and Bristol research on suicide prevention was notable, affecting individuals and others who might suffer from successful suicide, as well as offering financial, economic and other clear benefits.

A different, but innovative and impressive health-related study was Nottingham's work on healthy lives and community pharmacies (*Delivering public health services through community pharmacy*, Nottingham, UoA 3 — Pharmacy). As a result of the research, the role of the local pharmacist in the UK was reconfigured to expand the pharmacy's role in health and well-being, and, in doing so, enhancing the business and experience of pharmacists, and those working for them. The core to the change was pharmacists complementing the role of medical General Practitioners, taking on a number of services, such as vaccination, or first sight of certain conditions and, generally, being a point of consultation. As a result, communities could benefit from pharmacists' and their teams' expertise. One measure of this was a 140 per cent increase in stopping smoking. Meanwhile the pharmacists and their teams benefited themselves. Those benefits could be in terms of business and activity (increased income — in a quarter of cases, these were over 25 per cent increased prescription volume, and, in some cases, crucially, a 62 per cent rise in demand for public health services); or, the benefits could manifest themselves in job satisfaction (greater professional recognition and professional satisfaction, staff development and productivity). With 98 per cent of users recommending the service and 81 per cent judging it to be excellent, in addition to reductions in service costs to the NHS, this was a small and positive revolution in local healthcare.

In a quite different dimension of health-related research, the Sports and Exercise submissions from Bristol focused on improving everyday exercise, especially among young people. One study, which interestingly explicitly noted that underpinning research had featured in the RAE2008 submission (implying that it crossed the entry threshold), had innovatively provided the first objective metrics to show the importance of active travel to overall physical activity (subsequently picked up and replicated widely internationally) (*Changing policy and practice to increase active travel to school*, Bristol, UoA 26 — Sports

5 *Preventing Suicide in England: A cross-government outcomes strategy to save lives*, London: Department of Health, 2012.

and Exercise). That research had contributed to a range of national and international policy, planning and practice changes, initially led by Ashley Cooper from Bristol, which led to big increases in active travel among children, offering 'sustainable' improvements in both physical and mental health. In one case, in the UK, children's activity had 'almost doubled.' Cooperation with a non-governmental organisation in the UK, Sustrans, to develop safer routes and increased use of bicycles for 340,000 schoolchildren, led to an overall 80 per cent increase in those regularly riding to school. In another project in the US, there was a 64 per cent increase in children's walking to school and a 114 per cent increase in their cycling to school. The increase in active travel carried health benefits and, beyond this, it might be supposed, environmental and economic benefits.

A potentially even more exciting benefit concerned the health benefits of 'street play' (*Building new capacity to increase children's outdoor play*, Bristol, UoA 26 — Sports and Exercise). The Bristol research developed 'gold-standard' ways to measure the contribution that outdoor play can make both to children's independence and their physical activity and health. The research, showing that children would spend up to 30 per cent of their time outside engaged in moderate to vigorous physical activity, underpinned the development of adapting streets in Bristol for regular outdoor play, reintroducing a practice lost in the preceding decades. A key part of this transformation was legal reinterpretation that allowed wider use of temporary road closures that enabled more frequent and regular closures, rather than very occasional closures for exceptional purposes and limited to two, or three, in a year. As a result, a new instrument, a Temporary Street Play Order came into being, meaning that one application a year could cover the closing of streets between, say, 3.30 p.m. and 5.00 p.m. each afternoon (or at some other frequency), allowing children the scope to own the street for playing. With signage making clear the general prohibition of motor traffic in the given period, children could run and play in the streets with only the occasional vehicle allowed residential access to disturb them. The Bristol model was adopted nationally and internationally, following engagement, in the UK, with the Departments of Health and also Transport, as well as a partnership between the university, Play England and Playing Out CIC. By 2012, 304,200 'new play opportunities' had been created, benefiting children and health — and along with those opportunities, 400 volunteers and public servants benefited from training, 1,042 street play champion roles were developed and there was a 9 per cent increase in the number of children meeting national health guidelines for moderate to vigorous activity. Spread internationally, this research-based reversion to the patterns of earlier eras brought social, cultural and health transformations.

EvoFIT, a facial composite system, significantly enhanced police forces' arrests of criminal suspects, performing at least four times better than any previous system and achieving a minimum 25 per cent success rate, which in some instances reached a 60 per cent rate. Developed by Peter Hancock in the 1990s, the system was a mixture of software and procedures to help victims and witnesses to create likenesses of perpetrators' faces — and, so, to help police forces to identify and arrest (*EvoFIT: Applying Psychology To The Identification Of Criminals*, Stirling, UoA 4 — Psychology, Psychiatry and Neurology). The system involves a 'Holistic Cognitive Interview', in which it becomes possible to build on limited detail (which is usually the case) by getting witnesses to go beyond describing faces in terms not of physical features, and to recall and rate impressions of characteristics such as 'intelligence, selfishness and aggressiveness.' The system also included an animated caricature feature, to enable faces to come alive. As a result, highly identifiable composites emerged from the combination of physical feature description and holistic ratings. In the first case in EvoFIT's trial with the Lancashire police force, the composite produced from the interview with an 11-year-old girl, who had been sexually assaulted, was recognised by two members of the public and the culprit was apprehended and eventually convicted. This auspicious start was part of a trial in which six arrests resulted from 30 composites, an initial 20 per cent success rate. Other forces began to use the system — 14 of them in the UK, but it was also picked up in the US and extensively in Romania. And in great testimony to the innovative quality of the system, competitors incorporated it in their versions of composite systems, in operation with police forces not directly using EvoFIT.

In the examples of transformation introduced so far, and as is often assumed to be important, scale is taken as a measure of impact. Without doubt, there is good reason for that. But, in most of those cases, individuals were beneficiaries — and, in principle, a single individual's transformation could be the full scope of impact. To some extent, another one of the repertoire of distinctive cultural case studies from Newcastle (also involving research by Jackie Kay) points to this with one breathtaking quote from a single pupil about the enrichment of cultural life through poetry (*Poetry: Performance, Engagement and the Enrichment of Cultural Life*, Newcastle, UoA 29 — English):

> poetry fills your head … poetry would help you with your writing really … I think if you can get your head around poetry you can probably do all sorts of writing better …

This judgement could be applied to the value of any creative endeavour and the impact on just one individual can be immense. Of course, the power of this individual testimony is emblematic. While the reach and significance of one pupil is as great as it could be, this kind of benefit may be shared by many individuals — as is evident in the Newcastle study, which shows various types of difference made, whether teachers, or pupils, or healthcare professionals whose use of poetry in their work had brought inspiration back to that practice, those suffering from or combating racism in football,[6] or older people who can benefit from 'Ageing Creatively.' In each of these examples — and more — creativity is the key to individual well-being, a point radiantly made in this case study.

Given the point here, it is particularly salient that music and theatre submissions did well among the 4* ICSs. This could be composers writing new music, musicians playing it (in bands and orchestras), audiences benefiting from it — all showing a clear and innovative transformation. Examples include introducing a new awareness of potentially harmful noises (*Sanitary Sounds; listener-centred approach to the noise effects of ultra-rapid hand dryers on vulnerable subgroups*, Goldsmiths, UoA 35 — Music, Drama, Dance and Performing Arts). In this study, research involved innovative 'sound art' compositions and installations that gave healthy adults an interpretive sense of the discomfort suffered by certain categories of individual, for example, those with autistic spectrum disorders, dementia and sensory impairments, defining a new approach to performance and expanding horizons. A further study from Goldsmiths showed how ethnic musical traditions researched and preserved by John Baily were 'returned' to Afghanistan, after the Taliban period, in which they had been eradicated, while maintained in the diaspora, as the research confirmed (*Supporting Afghan music in the post-Taliban era*, Goldsmiths, UoA 35 — Music, Drama, Dance and Performing Arts). Goldsmiths was able to enhance Afghan culture in the country itself and transnationally in Afghan communities, with educational benefits including the creation of two schools, in Kabul and Herat, which schools led to expansive cultural enhancement, and opening music centres. Lois Weaver's one-woman blend of research, artistic practice and social engagement brought a core, radical and novel approach to non-hierarchical curation (*Transforming Publics and Participation through*

---

6 Sheffield United Football Club commissioned Kay to compose and read a poem at the start of a match as part of a campaign against racism in sport.

Practice, Queen Mary University of London, UoA 35 — Music, Drama, Dance and Performing Arts). This delivered a dazzling array of differences: directly to artists; to curators and programmers, which cascaded further to audiences; and to an international spread of audiences and communities, through participatory practices, with research on forms of public dialogue leading to her 'Public Address Systems.' This had wide impact, generating projects and events around the globe, in which diverse groups that experienced exclusion and marginalisation could contribute to serious discussions on crucial social questions, such as sexuality and the elderly, but also across the span of sexuality, ageing, human rights and emergent technologies. The transformative legacy of this work irradiated the ICS, in fold upon fold of detail.

Transformation is at the core of great impact, as the foregoing paragraphs have demonstrated. Whether high-level health policy and practice, or the feet of schoolchildren running and skipping in the street, and whether the quality of life of individuals suffering chronic disease, or of elderly individuals, this is the case. The examples show that notions of reach and significance perhaps rest more on a sense of salience — perhaps significance itself. From 111 ICSs considered for this analysis, only one,[7] perhaps, offered anything other than a clear and comprehensive sense making a real difference, in one way, or another. This is the universal quality in world-leading impact.

8. News media engagement and public engagement

The final characteristic in the analysis of world-leading impact studies from REF2014 is media engagement. This is the most challenging and, perhaps, surprising. This feature is included with caution for three reasons: it might well be rejected by some scholars and research and innovation functionaries; it runs counter to official definitions; and, last, while media engagement clearly emerged as a consistent and important trend in our study, it was not as extensive a presence as any of the other characteristics we have discussed. We weigh these issues and the conviction that it is right to include media (and other)

---

7 The one study that seemed notably less convincing than any of the others is discussed below in the context of media engagement, which was a strong feature in it (*Deradicalization and Jihadism: informing policy makers and informing public debate and understanding*, Exeter, UoA 27 — Area Studies).

engagement as our final characteristic, in the following paragraphs, before discussing some supporting examples.

Strong assertions that 'dissemination is not impact' and similar intonations in research council documentation clearly created a strong consciousness among those working in the councils and in similar roles, as well as among academics becoming versed in the new approach, that media engagement was of no real value — even though some academics sought such engagement and, where they did not do so, university hierarchies actively promoted it. Despite the overlap, these are discrete reasons. University managers might be influenced by 'the rules', but, there is no necessary reason for them to reject media engagement as a form of impact — all the more so, when there appears to be an 'everyday' sense that it is. Because of this, we approach the topic with openness. That those writing the rules stipulate that it is not impact could, independently, be a reason not to include it in our study. However, in line with the openness just indicated and also with that 'everyday' sense, there seems sound cause not to ignore the evidence that media engagement was prominent in many top-level studies (which also reinforces our identification of procedural impact as a type in Chapter 3).

We also exercise caution because there were large exceptions among the ICSs analysed, with 36 per cent of the ICSs making no evident reference to media. This makes it a far more weakly present characteristic than any of the others we have discussed. Yet, almost two thirds of the case studies did involve media engagement in some way. This is a substantial majority — one that it would be difficult to ignore, even if the preponderance does not compare with that in other features we have highlighted. The weaker salience might be sufficient reason to note this element, but then discard it. Equally, the scale to which it was found makes it hard to set aside. This is even more the case, if the degree to which it was unexpected is considered, given the strictures against taking media coverage to constitute impact. Precisely because it is so prominent, against expectations, this form of impact should be included. While the frequency with which it appeared might well be more than enough to justify its inclusion in our typology, the fact that this occurrence is despite and contrary to all guidance and expectations renders it unquestionably noteworthy.

Given the clear understanding established before REF2014 that 'media' attention and similar did not constitute impact, it is, then, more than a little surprising to find this characteristic to be of such importance. And, yet, with further reflection, it might not be such a surprise, if we consider that, as discussed in Chapter 3, most academics, when first confronted with the idea of impact, think entirely of media and public engagement. In light of this, it could be that those developing studies could not shake off the idea that this attribute was a big part of impact — even if, as was clear, making a big difference and other factors were involved. It could also suggest that, whatever the official and, even, more technical definitions of impact, news media interest is, in everyday understanding, taken to be impact.[8] We revisit this point in the Conclusion; but, for now, the clear balance of evidence, irrespective of other issues, confirms that media engagement merits inclusion in the typology.

The presence of media in case studies could take different forms. In a study such as Kingston's on the Hacked Off campaign, to which it contributed, in a curious way, it was inherent in it, throughout, because the news media constituted the focus of the study (Kingston University, *Impact on the Leveson Inquiry and press regulation in the UK*, UoA 29 — English Language and Literature). While news media did not constitute the focus of a London School of Economics and Political Science (LSE) study on rioting, youth disaffection, anti-social behaviour and policing, it was equally inherent, as the research and impact stemmed from the initiative of a major English newspaper, *The Guardian*, which was entwined in joint research and public engagement (*'Reading the Riots' and increasing public understanding*, LSE, UoA 22 — Social Work and Social Policy). In Swansea's BelVita study, media presence was through advertising (*The development of food items to benefit cognition and mood*, Swansea, UoA 4 — Psychology, Psychiatry and Neurology). In other cases, references could be made without much emphasis, in passing, or references might appear only in the supporting section. The former was instanced in studies that simply ran off a string of references to discussion of their work. For example, 'extensive worldwide media coverage in print, radio and television' — in *The Lancet*, on BBC national news and on the BBC Radio 4 *Today* programme (*Substantial changes in worldwide healthcare policy and the practice of joint replacement result from research into the failure rates of and systemic effects of metal-on-metal hip replacements*, Bristol, UoA 1 — Clinical Medicine); or, featured in more than 30 news articles across the world, citing Fox News, the *New York Daily News*, *The Irish Independent* and *Metro*, noting its 1.9 million

8 In this context, a point of comparison could be made with Bill Maley's excellent discussion of the term 'refugee', which has international and legal definition, but has an 'everyday' sense and use that is wider and, while overlapping with official versions, has a 'life of its own.' See William Maley, *What is a Refugee?* London: Hurst and Co., 2016, p. 38.

readership and online comments and sharing (*Informing public and policy debate about and improving understanding of the effects of cigarette and e-cigarette smoking*, UEL UoA 4 — Psychology, Psychiatry and Neurology). By contrast, other ICSs simply indicated media attention in the supporting references section (perhaps with brief assertion in the Evidence of Impact box). In one of these, in an alpha-beta list of supporting evidence, 'e' covered a variety of media examples, with the lead-in 'television and radio', which list was argued to provide evidence of 'raising public awareness' (*Translating research into novel immunotherapies delivers scientific and economic gains for the pharmaceutical/biotechnology sector in drug discovery*, Bristol, UoA 1 — Clinical Medicine). Two Imperial studies operated in a similar way, using an alpha-numerical list, under which 'E9', in one and 'E7, E8 and E9', in another, referenced media sources (*Case 2 — Device Applications of 3D Silicon Microstructures*; and *Case 3 — Ultra-Low-Power Electronics for Healthcare Applications*, Imperial College London, UoA 13 — Electrical Engineering).

Media engagement was particularly prominent in UoA 35 submissions, whether using reviews, as with Goldsmiths' *The ART of A.R.T*, or collaborating with community radio, in *History as Reconciliation — Non-Linear Narratives in African and African Diasporic Performance*, another Goldsmiths study (Goldsmiths, UoA 35 — Music, Drama, Dance and Performing Arts). Between reviews and other forms of coverage, media engagement, including considerable coverage on BBC Radios 3 and 4, in the UK, rippled through both of Southampton's studies in this category: *35–03 At Home with Music: Domestic Music-Making in Georgian Britain* and *The Music of Michael Finnissy* (Southampton, UoA 35 — Music, Drama, Dance and Performing Arts). News media also formed a notable part of *Empowering children online through literacy and safety initiatives* (LSE, UoA 36 — Communication, Cultural and Media Studies):

> National and international media reports of the research total 1800+, with Livingstone interviewed for the Daily Mail, Times, Guardian, Der Spiegel, Huffington Post, Panorama, Today, C4 News, GMTV Breakfast News, R4 Bringing Up Britain, You and Yours, Woman's Hour, Sky News and Newsnight. She contributed to Safer Internet Day, which the BBC estimates 10% UK population (14% of teens) heard in 2013, two thirds of whom said they would change their online behaviour as a result.

This densely referenced media coverage, amid the striking impacts described above, offered weighty confirmation of the range, reach and scope of the difference being made by the research, not only in terms of policy and practice, and benefit to young people, but also, arguably, in terms of public awareness and understanding.

Some studies provided a titled section on media and related engagement. These included a section on impact on media and politics in one of Durham's education studies. The study details research and development of a 'Toolkit' for evaluating the costs and benefits, and relative impact, of different teaching approaches in schools. Therefore, it is not surprising that educational media feature strongly in the section on media and politics, with 20 references. Interestingly, this section also includes the range of references to the Toolkit on a range of websites, from charities to publishers, highlighting the scope of impact in electronic media (*The Pupil Premium: building impact from evidence [Toolkit: ICS3]*, Durham, UoA 25 — Education). Another study with a dedicated section also made reference to specialist media, but did not do that in the dedicated section. This University of East London (UEL) study on the neuro-psychological effects of the Ecstasy drug — MDMA — contributed to understanding of potential harm, mainly through use of its research by the UK and US governments, as well as by practitioners. But, part of its contribution to understanding came through coverage in specialist venues (for example, *Medical News Today*), which was reported in the context of increasing the awareness of medical and health professionals. The contribution to wider understanding through television and radio coverage, including the BBC World Service, around the globe, and Channel 4 and ITN news broadcasts, as well as national press, in the UK, was presented separately (*Improving understanding among policy makers, the public and medical professionals of the potential harm that MDMA (Ecstasy) use may have on the neuro-psychological functioning of adults and babies*, UEL, UoA 4 — Psychology, Psychiatry and Neurology). This, perhaps, gave a focus to the entwined character of media engagement and public engagement, with the former perceived to be a chief vehicle (and, even, a proxy) for the latter.

Public engagement via news, current affairs and other communications media, was important in a number of studies. Stirling's EvoFIT study, already discussed, revealed the salience and reach of the research when the publication in *The Manchester Evening News* of the image developed using EvoFIT from the description by the sexually assaulted 11-year-old girl resulted in the two identifications and subsequent detention and eventual conviction of the culprit (*EvoFIT: Applying Psychology To The Identification Of Criminals*, Stirling, UoA 4 — Psychology, Psychiatry and Neurology). In addition to this important public engagement, however, the ICS also captured other media attention and prizes, referencing BBC Forum, the *Times Higher Education Supplement* and BBC1's *The One Show*. Public engagement via media was notable in other studies, such as Queen's University Belfast's work on transforming conflict in Northern Ireland. This research, which affected government policy and practice, and, most important, decisively shaped understanding of how and when flags should be used in public spaces, was reported extensively (with 226 articles) in both local news media in Northern Ireland and in national organs across the whole UK (*Displaying the Flag: Transforming Conflict in Northern Ireland*, Queen's University Belfast, UoA 24 — Anthropology and Development Studies). Warwick's agriculture submission (covering research and change, in which early use of antibiotics greatly reduced the prevalence of footrot in sheep) also recorded national and local media reporting, but, in addition, added specialist press to its reception — *Farmers Guardian, Farmers Weekly* and *The Sheep Farmer* (*Rapid Antibiotic Treatment Reduces the Prevalence of Lameness caused by Footrot in Sheep*, UoA 6 — Agriculture, Veterinary and Food Science). In all these cases, news media amplified research findings and enhanced impact, contributing to public engagement.

One study was unusual in relying almost entirely on the notion of impact through engagement: the Exeter case on de-radicalisation and jihadism (*De-radicalisation and Jihadism: informing policy makers and informing public debate and understanding*, Exeter, UoA 27 — Area Studies). Aside from clear references to citations in a US counter-terrorism White Paper and a United Nations Economic and Social Commission for West Asia report, most of the ICS is surprising in resting on assertion and evidence that anyone heeding the 'dissemination not impact' line discussed in Chapter 2 would not have used — or would have done so expecting the case study to be deemed to be fairly weak. While two references just noted are notable, the ICS as a whole reads like a weak study, indeed — and certainly not as something that might be expected to gain the top rating. With one part of this ICS about 'informing policy makers' and the other about 'informing public debate', the evidence was more about dissemination. The claimed impact on policy makers involved reporting presentations by Dr. Omar Ashour to the Foreign and Commonwealth Office and representatives from other UK government departments and to practitioners, or researchers, aside from the references already indicated. The contribution that 'raised' public awareness rested entirely on heavy media engagement — involving 400 interviews in various news outlets, including various BBC outputs, CNN and al-Jazeera, as well as print and online media. Taken together, because this study gained the top rating, despite the characteristics of something that might be expected to be weaker impact, the inference must be that, despite the official positions taken by research councils (and institutional professionals) before REF2014, recording dense public and media engagement could add up to something reviewers would regard as world leading.

The single study from the 16 that we originally examined that did not reference news media in any way was Leicester's work devising ways beyond mere attendance numbers to measure and evaluate benefits to museum visitors (Leicester, *Measuring Visitor Learning*, UoA 36 — Communication, Cultural and Media Studies). The model of Generic Learning Outcomes captured individuals' experience under five headings: knowledge and understanding; skills; attitudes and values; enjoyment, inspiration and creativity; and activity, progression and behaviour. This reflected the range of experiences a museum visitor — or a visitor to any other kind of cultural encounter — might have and, as the study indicated, had reach into other areas in which audiences, or visitors, were an important element, such as the BBC and the National Trust. This is an example of an ICS that clearly did not need media engagement and, so far as could be detected, there was none, yet, the study was one in which there might well have been; it is not hard to imagine the study supplemented by news reports, had they been (sought and) available.

The same could be said of other studies. These included *Devolution and the Creation of a New Language Law Regime in Wales* (Cardiff, UoA 28 — Modern Languages), which resulted, inter alia, in devolution of language responsibility from the UK Government in London, to the Welsh Government in Cardiff, and, subsequently, to the latter's committing to a 'national standard' of bi-lingual public services. They also incorporated both *Changing policy and practice to increase active travel to school* and *Building new capacity to increase children's outdoor play* (Bristol, UoA 26 — Sports and Exercise), which were discussed already above and for which, in many respects, it was surprising that either there had been no news coverage, or attention was not drawn to it. Other instances include: the award-winning new visitor experience that transformed Hampton Court Palace (*Cultural and economic impact on Hampton Court Palace from research-based visitor experience*, Kingston, UoA 29 — English); all of Oxford's studies in Social Work — *Improving evidence-based policy and programming for AIDS-affected children in Sub-Saharan Africa, Regulating labour immigration: Labour markets, welfare states and public policy, Targeting resources and interventions in deprived areas using small area level indices of deprivation in the UK and South Africa* and *Reducing child anti-social behaviour through effective parenting interventions: international impact on policy, practitioners and families* (Oxford, UoA 22 — Social Work and Social Policy); and some of the LSE's studies in the same UoA, but not all — *Better measures of fuel poverty, Child protection: improving practice* and *Shaping the financing of long-term care* all contained no media references, while two others, *Improving policy and practice to promote better health* and *Re-igniting R&D for antibiotics*, used news media support and impact.

In other studies with no media engagement, the absence made elementary sense. The nature of some studies, such as Exeter's example built around Gareth Stansfield's sensitive contributions to UK and international policy and engagement in Iraq were simply not appropriate for news coverage (*Political Dynamics in post-2003 Iraq*, Exeter, UoA 27 — Area Studies). Similarly, Cardiff's engineering work on nuclear waste involved sensitivity not appropriate for media attention (*Engineering Solutions for High Level Nuclear Waste Disposal*, UoA 14 — Civil and Construction Engineering). In addition, many of those with no media reporting were found among studies on medicine, where a focus on clinical outcomes and, in some cases, perhaps, the commercial sensitivity of drug and therapeutic development might make such engagement irrelevant. Examples include a handful of the Bristol studies in medicine (*New businesses, commercial investment and adoption of new technology result from antigen-specific peptide immunotherapy development*; *Minimal residual disease assessment in acute lymphoblastic leukaemia allows safe individualisation of chemotherapy and reduction of treatment toxicity*; and *Lower risks to patients, advances in international practice and substantial resource savings result from 'beating heart' off-pump coronary artery bypass surgery*, Bristol, UoA 1 — Clinical Medicine), as well several of those from Dundee, in the same category (*Spironolactone as a Treatment to extend life in Heart Failure Patients*; *New Approaches to Drug and Chemical Safety Assessment*; *Filaggrin — the major predisposing gene for atopic disease and a target for stratified therapeutic intervention*; and *BNP as a Diagnostic and Risk Stratifying Test in Cardiology*, Dundee, UoA 1 — Clinical Medicine). Media and public engagement, therefore, were certainly not necessary to achieving 4* impact grading, even if, sometimes, evidence of them might well have supplemented otherwise excellent material. However, it is equally clear that media and public engagement cannot necessarily be excluded as a characteristic of high-level impact. Indeed, we are struck, given the 'media coverage is not impact' mantra and the 'dissemination is not impact' tone set before REF2014, that the 4* studies drew, often quite significantly, on media engagement and other public dissemination activities, in particular, as an indication of reach.

This cements our sense that media engagement and contributions to public awareness merit a place in the typology we have presented here. It is evident that media and public engagement can be a significant aspect of impact, no matter the more puritan views of some. Not only was it a feature of almost two thirds of the 4* impact case studies analysed here, but it was also, more or less, the essence of one study. That study could be seen as weak impact, in the eyes of some, reading it with the formulae of research officialdom guiding their vision. However, it seems that the 'everyday' sense of impact felt by many scholars should cautiously be shared. It is that sense of the phenomenon that may be presumed to lie behind the prevalence of media and public engagement in a strong majority of ICSs. And the evidence appears to be that one panel clearly shared that 'everyday' sense when judging case studies.

The characteristics of world-leading research, exceptions and limitations

Given the limitations on our study, addressed above, it is still possible that these findings might theoretically have a provisional character and, so, might also require revision, at some stage. However, having reviewed all 111 of the impact case studies known certainly to have been evaluated as world leading in REF2014, we judge that the consistency of features identified, to date, gives a reliable foundation for understanding what constitutes a 4* impact case study.

This understanding must be leavened with some necessary caveats, even though they give a very good sense of 4* ICSs. First, this analysis does not mean that a 4* ICS must conform to and share all of these characteristics — a 4* ICS could also take a different form. Indeed, as we conclude this part of our analysis, it is appropriate to mention the exception to almost everything above. This is the remarkable ICS in Psychology from Birkbeck College on eye tracking and the restoration of the John Martin masterpiece *The Destruction of Herculaneum* in conjunction with the Tate Gallery (*A vision of destruction restored: Using eyetracking to guide the restoration of John Martin's 'The Destruction of Pompeii and Herculaneum' (1821)*, Birkbeck College, UoA 4 — Psychology, Psychiatry and Neurology). This was, in many respects, perhaps the most outstanding and unusual of all 111 case studies. It was based around one researcher, working on one painting with one institution — a set of singularities not found anywhere else. Beyond this, the brilliant use of eye-tracking technology enabled the restoration of a seriously damaged and long-unseen major painting in a novel manner, that would make it not only the star of the show, but returned to permanent display. The study also bore the striking characteristics of a focus on cultural impact, rather than policy, or patents, and also the adoption of visual evidence in presenting its narrative — features that occurred satisfyingly in an attractive minority of other ICSs, but not enough of them to warrant discrete inclusion in our study.

This Birkbeck case is an exception that very much makes the point that impact does not have to conform to any particular recipe, while arguably confirming the 'rule' that it is likely to feature several of them. Even such a highly distinctive study as this exemplified innovation and transformation, researcher engagement and beneficiary investment, as well as critical approval in news media. In general, then, all stories of impact will show some of these characteristics.

In addition, regarding caveats, secondly, the typology we have presented is not necessarily a template, or recipe, for a 4* ICS. It might well be a useful framework to consider — we judge that it is. To some extent, these features will not change, nor will the value in having them be completely removed. But, leaving aside that each case is, in the end, *sui generis*, as beauty is in the eye of the beholder, so the 'evaluator's eye', in Gemma Derrick's great term, might regard matters differently — especially, given the socialisation and groupthink exposed in her analysis (described in Chapter 2).

The value in our analysis rests on the overwhelming sense, from close critical evaluation of all the impact case studies known to be at 4* level, that the consistency of the eight characteristics identified is reliable. The 111 ICSs did not quite universally reveal all eight characteristics, but, almost all had almost all of them. As a framework for understanding the presentation of world-leading research impact in the REF exercise, our analysis offers much. And while the analysis could be said to be limited because of the REF focus, it should also be noted that, however far the evaluation exercise and its template are a factor in shaping the material, and so the findings, it is absolutely reasonable to suppose that the features identified in REF narratives are, independently, the self-same characteristics that serious impact could be expected to reveal, wholly irrespective of the particular form of the narrative requirement demanded by the REF exercise. It may, therefore, be taken cautiously as a guide to 4* impact and its presentation.

As we have argued above, the analysis signals the right direction for achieving and presenting 4* research impact and, in some ways, offers something of an answer to the bold question posed by Mark Reed and his colleagues involved in Fast Track Impact: what makes a 4* impact case study? The work by Reed and Fast Track Impact, exposed in Chapter 5, provides a completely different, but complementary understanding of how to achieve 4* research impact, albeit that it, inevitably, also has limitations, as indicated in that chapter and in Chapter 1. However, informed by that research on use of language and our own more 4*-focused framework, those exploring the realm of world-leading impact and its presentation in impact case studies should be better placed to address the question.

8 Conclusion

We began this study with the question of the relative failure of Politics and International Studies in REF2014. We return to it in this Conclusion, in light of the analysis of 4* impact in the preceding three chapters, as well as the examination of impact and review of the field and its potential, in earlier chapters. First, we reflect on the notion of impact and recapitulate a typology of impact, involving instrumental, conceptual, capacity-building and procedural elements. The last of these is a novel contribution, identified in our research, alongside the salience of media and public engagement. However, this runs counter to dominant understandings of research impact, whether in the Research Excellence Framework (REF), or at UK research councils. Despite this and also a somewhat nebulous and uncertain character, we introduce this aspect, albeit with caution and readiness for further considerations, given our findings for top impact studies and the re-ported understanding of impact among researchers. In the following section, we re-present an analysis of that which constitutes 'world-leading' research impact and how to achieve it — the quest for 4*s, as well as reflections on the possibilities and limitations of our research. Reinforcing the impact typology, this includes our finding that news and media formed a consistent element in 4* impact case studies (ICSs). Finally, after revisiting the earlier discussion of impact in international affairs prior to the introduction of the official impact agenda, we conclude by considering 'why POLIS fails' — confirming the suspicion of underperformance.

Instrumental, conceptual, capacity-building and procedural impact, and the media issue

Impact is a complex problem in various ways. It can never be assumed that it will be achieved. To begin with, researchers often differ in their commitment to making a difference in the world, with some believing that engagement with stakeholders and the real world sullies academic integrity and ivory tower purity. Beyond this, there is the reality that impact is to a considerable extent a matter of serendipity. Even with potential and desire, it may be that findings simply emerge at the right time and in the right context for them to have impact. Chance is important, no matter how impact might be accomplished otherwise. The prospect of impact is stronger, of course, where potential beneficiaries are engaged from the very outset. Yet, even in these cases, no guarantee is available. Many things can happen: those engaging might change; research findings may be disappointing and of little relevance.

Moreover, evidence is always an issue — although, as seen in much of this volume, some excellent material supported case studies. Even where impact has clearly occurred, sometimes the evidence might remain confidential and so cannot be used to confirm it — as noted in some of the examples in Chapters 6 and 7, sometimes evidence was redacted, perhaps, for commercial reasons. In other instances, it is possible that, even where impact might be known to have occurred, those who could confirm it, or offer evidence, simply will not do so — whatever their reasons, ethically, they have the right to withhold whatever evidence they might possess.

Finally, impact can generally only be clearly demonstrated through empirical description and interpretation of specific examples. None the less, a synthetic interpretation is possible and it can be conceptualised and translated into the quadripartite typology of instrumental, conceptual, capacity building and procedural that we present in Chapter 3. Instrumental impact occurs where practice is changed, as was the case with the examples of Economic Community of West African States (ECOWAS) youth policy and UK inter-agency operations, and military learning and adaptation focused on the UK campaign in Afghanistan, in Chapter 4. Conceptual impact involves a change in thinking. Many examples of this could be seen throughout Chapters 6 and 7, but could also be taken to characterise, the way the New Security Challenges Radicalisation and Violence (NSCRV) programme, discussed in Chapter 4, reframed 'radicalisation' discourse. Capacity-building impact involves the translation of research into the spread of new knowledge and understanding, taken forward through training and adoption of content and practice. One example of this was the amazing spread of 'street play', as discussed in Chapter 7.

While the first three of these types of impact are relatively accepted in official approaches, procedural impact is an innovation. As such, it is borne out by both the 'everyday' understanding held by most researchers and practitioners, and also by our analysis. Procedural impact could possibly be re-framed as one of the other forms. Yet, there is sufficient evidence that researchers and practitioners sense a form of impact that does not necessarily quite fit the other terms. This could be seen in partnerships, such as those formed as a result of conducting research on Muslim communities in West London and the West Midlands, while, as noted, research could have some influence on strategic defence and security thinking, without actually reaching the level of conceptual change in the UK Strategic Defence and Security Review.

While clear 'conceptual' impact results in changed thinking, then 'procedural' impact remains at a cathectic level. Those involved 'feel' that research engagement has been beneficial, without being able to articulate, or characterise, impact beyond this. While being affected in some diffuse way could just be seen as 'conceptual', there are clearly times where researchers and stakeholders believe that there has been value, albeit amorphous and lacking definition.

Another dimension of this form of impact is media engagement and contributions to public awareness, which may form part of procedural impact, despite the more puritanical views some might hold. This was a feature of almost two thirds of the 4* impact case studies analysed in this book and cannot be ignored. The 'everyday' sense of impact felt by so many should be embraced, even if cautiously. Certainly, the burden of evidence suggests that those evaluating impact shared that 'everyday' sense.

How to get 4*, world-leading impact

In the course of the preceding chapters, we explored how to identify 'world-leading' research, in terms of the REF2014 exercise. Chapter 5 encompassed a critical exposition of valuable evidence of how to achieve high-scoring research impact, based on discourse analysis of 3* and 4* ICSs. This research by the Fast Track Impact team did not isolate the 4* level, so could not be a complete prescription. But, it provides some indication and complements our own research, presented in Chapters 6 and 7. Those chapters constitute a unique analysis of 'world-leading' (4*) research in REF2014. It is based on examination of 111 impact studies, from REF2014, found in 20 out of the 36 units of assessment (UoA) and in 35 discrete submissions in those 20 UoAs, and known with certainty to have been rated 4*. The eight features consistently identified in that sample represent well-founded understanding of 4*, 'world-leading' impact: 1. long-term research and impact context; 2. quality/significant research funding; 3. clear engagement/an embedded role in implementation/researcher-practitioner unity; 4. resource/financial commitment to impact; 5. quotes as evidence and presentation; 6. breadth/range/multiplicity/cumulative effect; 7. creating something new/transformative for beneficiaries; 8. news media engagement and public engagement.

While these features spread across all the 4* studies, there was no particular correlation between either institution, or unit of assessment, in that span. The highest percentage of 100 per cent 4* submissions came in UoA 20 — Law and, at 7.46 per cent, was not especially high. Ironically, Law also had the highest percentage of submissions that failed to achieve any 4* impact — over half of all submissions (50.75 per cent). Clinical Medicine, perhaps, performed best overall, with the highest percentage of 100 per cent 4* submissions and the lowest percentage of submissions with no 4* studies. And, while no firm conclusion can be drawn, it is possible to observe that, unlike Medicine, some more applied disciplines that might be expected to do well because of seeming utility to society secured relatively poor outcomes (such as General Engineering, Informatics and Architecture). More broadly, there was at least one university that achieved complete success in 20 out of the 36 units of assessment. However, in one fifth of those 20 — that is, 4 out of the 20 — four submissions in each UoA reached a perfect outcome. These were UoAs 4 (Psychology), 22 (Social Work and Social Policy), 29 (English) and 35 (Music, Drama, Dance and Performing Arts). That means that almost half of the 100 per cent world-leading submissions — 16 out of the 35 that gained 100 per cent 4* ratings — occurred in only four UoAs.[1] This might reflect the nature of those subject areas, or it might reflect a more generous approach by those panels. Yet, its real significance is hard to determine. It might simply be no more than a reflection of quality in those particular submissions. Certainly, it is difficult reliably to infer any correlation between subject and score, given that 2014 was the first time the impact exercise was carried out and these are the only results available.

Similarly, the evidence does not indicate any significant correlation between universities and complete success. Very few universities managed to achieve more than one 100 per cent 4* submission. LSE, Cardiff, Swansea and York each managed two, leaving Bristol as the only institution to get a perfect outcome in four UoAs. A stronger

1 See Annex 1.

correlation can be found between particular universities and consistently poor impact scores, however. Some 67 different institutions had four or more submissions with no 4* impact; and 22 of these had at least double that number failing to register any 4* impact. The 'new universities' from the post-1990 era dominate these groupings — though we must recall that some from this category had 100 per cent 4* submissions (Bedfordshire, Hertfordshire, Kingston, UEL). The universities of Chester and Greenwich achieved the joint highest number of no 4* submissions, each with 13 submissions. Generally, this is probably to be expected, reflecting the difference between more and less research-intensive universities. It might also be a reflection of the generally smaller size of submissions from those institutions — certainly, there was a small, but notable, difference in the mean number of studies per 100 per cent world-leading submission (3.14 ICSs) and those with zero impact at that level (2.26 ICSs). This perhaps denotes a difference between units submitting the minimum number of case studies required and those with stronger research environments, suggesting, perhaps, that the latter were somewhat stretched — as, we could speculate, might have been far larger sub-missions, given the mean of just over 3 case studies per submission, suggesting that it might become harder consistently to have top-level impact once a submission goes beyond 3 studies.

Perhaps the strongest inference on impact that could be drawn from the REF2014 exercise was a prima facie approximation of overall performance across the four main panels. Main Panel A did the best, by a considerable distance, with both the highest percentage of 100 per cent 4* submissions (2.8 per cent) and the lowest percentage of submissions that failed to hit that level (19.88 per cent). Main Panel B trailed the other main panels, with only 0.49 per cent achieving a 100 per cent world-leading submission. In Main Panel C, however, it is notable that 'social science' minus the humanities subjects included in the panel's purview, had the worst performance of all: completely world leading was only 0.36 per cent; and the failure to achieve any 4* score was second greatest, at 33.69 per cent. Curiously, while a varied range of subjects secured top scores, there was a concentration of UoAs in Natural Sciences and Engineering that failed to secure any 100 per cent 4* submissions and also failed to hit the world-leading mark at all — despite the full house success in Electrical Engineering for Imperial. The other main panels all had a roughly similar proportion of submissions with no top-level impact — each around 30 per cent.

As the first research audit to seek to measure impact, REF2014 only gave scope for limited conclusions. It was difficult to make explicit links between subject and score, but it was also clear that some subjects outperformed others, especially at the main panel level, where Main Panel A easily did best, while Natural Sciences and Engineering, Main Panel B, scored consistently poorly. Overall, as we have outlined, the clearest points of inference are the eight characteristics of world-leading impact identified at the start of this section and in Chapters 6 and 7.

Why POLIS 'fails'

International politics is a field of study with its very roots entwined in notions of impact. Yet, there was seemingly underperformance in POLIS — Politics and International Studies — in REF2014, in terms of impact, identified at the outset of this book and given contextual discussion in Chapter 4. That context showed that there was international devotion to, and achievement of, impact, as well as some notable achievement and potential generated under research council programmes, before the appearance of the official agenda. Yet, the picture was uneven, with potential missed, or impact simply absent. As we saw in Chapter 4, there was some underperformance and disappointment in relation to major funding programmes prior to the REF impact era. Yet, REF2014, while confirming unevenness, including some high points, was really a failure in international affairs when considered against the other UoAs.

It might be that 'why POLIS fails' is merely a reflection of the poor performance of social science, overall, on the impact test. As noted in the previous section, when isolated from subjects with more of a humanities focus, social sciences were the lowest scoring for impact, overall, in REF2014. This is all the more striking, if we understand that the pitiful mean outcome of 0.36 per cent at 4* comes from a sample that includes as many as 11 of the 35 submissions that gained 100 per cent world-leading scores for impact, that fell under Main Panel C, social sciences. It speaks darkly for the general weakness in social sciences that the measly average of 0.36 per cent of ICSs at 4* is a mean figure derived from a total sample that included so many excellent, full-house, 4* achievements — almost one third of the total of 35 submissions that we know achieved that top level completely. That means that the social science average, overall, must be inflated by those high-scoring submissions, suggesting extremely poor performance, generally. For Politics and International Studies, that picture could be worse, given the absence of any completely successful impact submission in that UoA.

There are five potential explanations for the failure of POLIS. First, as noted in the Introduction, it could be that a focus on studying policy worlds and decision-making means that process is the focus, rather than content, which content might make a difference. Therefore, concrete change is likely rare, if not unachievable. Secondly, also as noted in the Introduction, another factor may well be that the type of research that makes it through the peer review process, with an emphasis on theoretical and methodological questions, might well not have been aligned with types of knowledge useful to those producing policy. To be of sufficient interest and use for practitioners to engage with it, at all, the research must be of relevance, in the first place. Some of the responsibility, therefore, likely might lie with some of the researchers themselves.[2] Thirdly, in a similar vein, our research showed that many scholars sceptically believed that policy makers and practitioners were unlikely to use research findings, particularly, because of the supposedly 'reflexive' and theoretical character of research, rather than its being empirically focused — even if, in reality, as seen through the REF2014 exercise, there might actually have been far more usage than often assumed.[3] This unevenness seemed to translate into outcomes from REF2014, where there was no 100 per cent 4* submission.

However, even with this unevenness registered, a consideration of the wider REF environment suggests more was at play than simply POLIS failing to realise impact at the level that might be expected. The two remaining explanations for this might well be the sub-panel itself. Fourthly, then, it seems likely that those tasked with evaluating the field tended to define 'impact' in limited terms of policy, giving less weight to cultural, legal, social or other forms of impact. Finally, our examination of top-rated impact submissions potentially brought into question some of the sub-panel's judgements, notably, the suspicion of meanness and self-inflicted harm. This is reaffirmed in our study of world-leading impact, which demonstrates that complete success was possible, in theory, and was, indeed, accomplished in 20 different UoAs. In this light, Essex offers a clear and easily manageable

---

2 This observation is one originally made by a couple of very senior figures in the field, confidentially.

3 This seems particularly true of those working in 'critical IR.' There is some evidence, however, to suggest a shift in this respect, as scholars that might be labelled as 'critical', albeit based in solid empirical research, increasingly came to be engaged with policy. Roger Mac Ginty's 'Everyday Peace Indicators', taken up by the United Nations as a means of measuring the success of peace processes, offers an example of this.

example. It was already rated highly by the panel — at 80 per cent, easily second highest in the UoA. Yet, looking at the two impact studies, it is hard to see anything that clearly makes them weaker than the 4* case studies critically appraised in this book. Indeed, one has all eight of the characteristics identified in our research; the other only seven of them (missing the news media aspect, ironically; the very focus of the first study). Moreover, the weakest of our 111-strong sample of 4* case studies was probably weaker than either of these.

Whatever the reasons, there is a firm impression of under-performance. As we have discussed, one reason might be the nature of the subject and forms of knowledge. It might also be, in another part, because work with greater impact potential was not especially fa-voured in peer review and funding exercises. And, finally, some of the explanation may be found in a relative 'mean spiritedness' about the field in the past, where, as recognised, the discipline was prone to self-inflicted wounds — reflected in the REF sub-panel. Whatever the precise balance in explanation, it is hard not to conclude that, in terms of REF, there was likely parsimony in the assessments made. While 4* impact was clearly possible, including the 100 per cent world-leading outcomes achieved in many other areas, Politics and International Studies failed.

Annex 1

100 per cent 4* impact: UoAs and institutions

1.	UoA 01	Clinical Medicine	Bristol, Dundee
2.	UoA 02	Public Health, Health Services and Primary Care	Bristol
3.	UoA 03	Allied Health Professions, Dentistry, Nursing and Pharmacy	Nottingham
4.	UoA 04	Psychology, Psychiatry and Neurology	Birkbeck, Stirling, Swansea, UEL
5.	UoA 06	Agriculture, Veterinary and Food Science	Warwick
6.	UoA 13	Electrical and Electronic Engineering, Metallurgy and Materials	Imperial
7.	UoA 14	Civil and Construction Engineering	Cardiff
8.	UoA 18	Economics and Econometrics	Bristol
9.	UoA 20	Law	Ulster
10.	UoA 22	Social Work and Social Policy	LSE, Oxford, UCL, York
11.	UoA 23	Sociology	York
12.	UoA 24	Anthropology and Development Studies	Queen's University Belfast
13.	UoA 25	Education	Durham, Sheffield
14.	UoA 26	Sports and Exercise Sciences, Leisure and Tourism	Bristol
15.	UoA 27	Area Studies	Exeter
16.	UoA 28	Modern Languages and Linguistics	Cardiff
17.	UoA 29	English Language and Literature	Bedfordshire, Kingston, Newcastle, Swansea
18.	UoA 30	History	Hertfordshire

| 19. | UoA 35 | Music, Drama, Dance and Performing Arts | QMUL, Southampton, RNCM, Goldsmiths |
| 20. | UoA 36 | Communication, Cultural and Media Studies, Library and Information Management | Leicester, LSE |

Selected bibliography

Davies, Huw, Nutley, Sandra and Walter, Isabel, 'Why "Knowledge Transfer" is Misconceived for Applied Social Research', *Journal of Health Services Research & Policy* Vol. 13 No. 3 2008.

Derrick, Gemma, *The Evaluators' Eye: Impact Assessment and Academic Peer Review*, Cham: Palgrave Macmillan, 2018.

Details of the call for proposals to the *Beyond Text: Performances, Sounds, Images, Objects Programme Follow on Funding Scheme*, AHRC, 2010 October.

Duke, K., 'Evidence-based Policy Making? The Interplay between Research and the Development of Prison Drugs Policy', *Criminal Justice* Vol. 1 No. 3 2001.

Ekblom, P., 'From the Source to the Mainstream is Uphill: The Challenge of Transferring Knowledge of Crime Prevention Through Replication, Innovation and Anticipation' in Tilley, N., ed., *Analysis for Crime Prevention*, Morrisey, NY: Criminal Justice Press, 2002.

ESRC, *ESRC Strategic Plan 2009–14: Delivering Impact Through Social Science*, Swindon: ESRC, No Date.

ESRC, *Taking Stock: A Summary of ESRC's Work to Evaluate the Impact of Research on Policy and Practice*, No Place: ESRC, 2009 February.

King's College London and Digital Science, *The Nature, Scale and Beneficiaries of Research Impact: An Initial Analysis of Research Excellence Framework (REF) 2014 Impact Case Studies, Research Report 2015/01*, Prepared for the Higher Education Funding Council of England, Higher Education Funding Council for Wales, Scottish Funding Council, Department of Employment and Learning Northern Ireland, Research Councils UK and the Wellcome Trust, London: HEFCE, 2015.

Knott, J. and Wildavsky, A., 'If Dissemination is the Solution, What is the Problem?' *Knowledge: Creation, Diffusion, Utilization* Vol. 1 No. 4 1980.

Landry, R., Amara, N. and Lamari, M., 'Climbing the Ladder of Research Utilization', *Science Communication* Vol. 22 No. 4 2001.

Landry, R., Amara, N. and Lamari, M., 'Utilization of Social Research Knowledge in Canada', *Research Policy* Vol. 30 No. 2 2001.

Nutley, Sandra M., Walter, Isabel and Davies, Huw T.O., *Using Evidence: How Research Can Inform Public Services*, Bristol: Policy Press, 2007.

Reichard, Bella, Reed, Mark S., Chubb, Jenn, Hall, Jowett, Ged, Lucy and Peart, Alisha, 'Pathways to a Top-scoring Impact Case Study', *Palgrave Communications* (in press at the time of writing).

Research Excellence Framework impact pilot exercise: *Findings of the Expert Panels: A Report to the UK Higher Education Funding Bodies by the Chairs of the Impact Pilot Panels*, Higher Education Funding Council for England, 2010 November.

Smith, Katherine and Stewart, Ellen, 'We Need to Talk about Impact: Why Social Policy Academics Need to Engage with the UK's Research Impact Agenda', *Journal of Social Policy* Vol. 46 No. 1 2017, pp.109–127.

Smith, Simon, Ward, Vicky and House, Allan, '"Impact" in the Proposals for the UK's Research Excellence Framework: Shifting the Boundaries of Academic Autonomy', *Research Policy* Vol. 40 No. 1 2011.

Spalek, Basia, el-Awa, Salwa, McDonald, Laura Zahra, *Police-Muslim Engagement and Partnerships for the Purposes of Counter-Terrorism: An Examination*, AHRC-ESRC Religion and Society Programme Summary Report, 2008 18 November.

'Special Issue: The Impact Agenda in British Higher Education', *British Politics* Vol. 13 No. 3, September 2018.

Sunesson, S. and Nilsson, K., 'Explaining Research Utilization: Beyond "Functions"', *Knowledge: Creation, Diffusion, Utilization* Vol. 10 No. 2 1988.

Weiss, C.H., 'The Many Meanings of Research Utilization', *Public Administration Review* Vol. 39 No. 5 1979.

Woodhead, Linda, *AHRC/ESRC Religion and Society Programme for 2007: University of Lancaster End of Year Report*, AHRC/ESRC, 2007.

Woodhead, Linda, with Catto, Rebecca, *'Religion or Belief': Identifying Issues and Priorities*, Equality and Human Rights Commission Research Report 48, Manchester: Equality and Human Rights Commission, 2009.

Wooding, Steven, Nason, Edward, Klautzer, Lisa, Rubin, Jennifer, Hanney, Stephen, Grant, Jonathan, *Policy and Practice Impacts of Research Funded by the Economic and Social Research Council: A Case Study of the Future of Work Programme, Approach and Analysis*, Cambridge: Rand Europe, 2007.

Index